The Chef in a TRUCK

Text by Éric Nebot
Recipes by François Perret, with the exception of those on pages 60 and 78

Photographs: © Bernhard Winkelmann / Flammarion for pages 10, 16, 19, 21, 23, 25, 63, 70–71, 92–93, 107, 109, 126–27, 128–29, 144–45, 147, 151, 153, 155, 161, 163, 165, 167, 169
© Ashley Maxwell for page 61
© Pascal Shirley for page 79
All of the other photographs: © 2021 *The Chef in a Truck*

Design: Delphine Delastre
Editor: Ryma Bouzid

English Edition
Editorial Director: Kate Mascaro
Editor: Helen Adedotun
Translated from the French by Magda Schmit
Copyediting: Wendy Sweetser
Typesetting: Gravemaker+Scott
Proofreading: Rachel Doux
Production: Louisa Hanifi and Christelle Lemonnier
Color Separation: IGS, L'Isle d'Espagnac
Printed in Slovenia by DZS Grafik

Simultaneously published in French as *The Chef in a Truck: La Fabuleuse odyssée culinaire d'un pâtissier français en Californie*
© Flammarion, S.A., Paris, 2021

English-language edition
© Flammarion, S.A., Paris, 2021

87, quai Panhard et Levassor
75647 Paris Cedex 13

editions.flammarion.com

21 22 23 3 2 1

ISBN: 978-2-08-024853-4

Legal Deposit: 10/2021

FRANÇOIS PERRET
Pastry Chef at the Ritz Paris
with **ÉRIC NEBOT**

The Chef in a TRUCK

The Fabulous Culinary Odyssey of a French Pastry Chef in California

Flammarion

CONTENTS

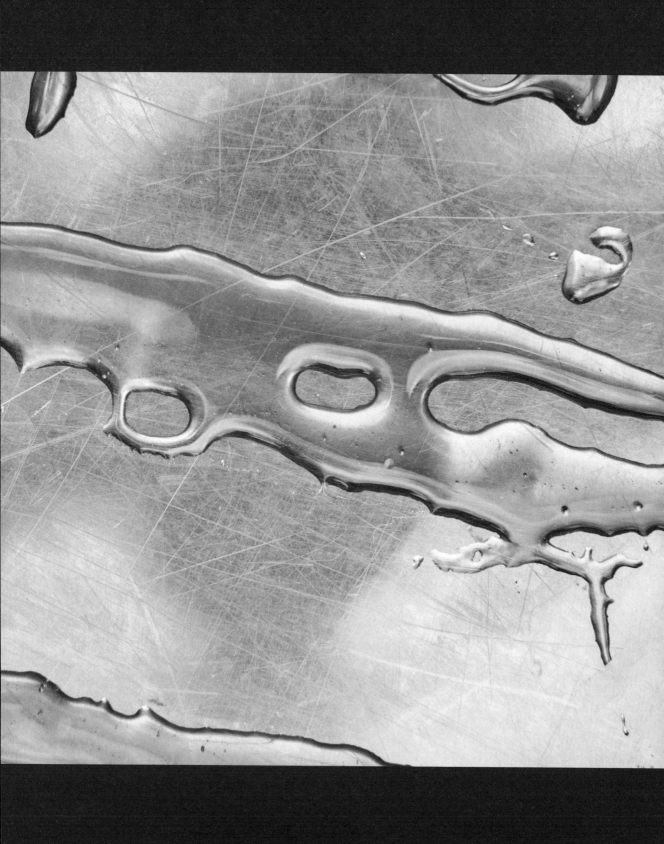

MY GRANDMOTHER AND I: A TALE OF LOVE AND CUISINE

It was love imparted through taste. The love of flavorsome food. The love of passing down knowledge, of cooking, relishing, talking, and sharing. Cooking was my grandmother's unbreakable bond with others, with her family, and with me.

Éric Nebot

Baking was always an important part of our relationship. When I was very young, I learned to make my first cake with her. It was a yogurt cake, and the recipe was extremely simple thanks to the foolproof memory aid of 1-2-3-4.

Tip 1 pot of plain yogurt into a mixing bowl and then, using the empty yogurt pot, add:
1 pot of oil
2 pots of sugar
3 pots of flour
4 eggs
1 tablespoon of baking powder
1 pinch of salt (never forget the salt, even in cakes and pastries!)
And the finely grated zest of 1 lemon
Stir everything together until well mixed and transfer to a cake pan.
Bake in an oven preheated to 350°F (180°C/ Gas Mark 4) for 45 minutes.
And that's it!

When my grandmother passed away, I was left with an unimaginable void in my life that I felt a vital need to fill. I did this through a love of good food. It was as if taste had become a divine means of communication between us.

In 2017, I went to live in Los Angeles. The city's culinary culture is vibrant. The climate provides the perfect conditions for a wide range of high-quality fruits and vegetables throughout the year. There are also excellent pastries made using superior ingredients— larger than life pastries that are generous and beautiful. It's a vast city where you can often enjoy great food, when you know the right places to go.

Living as an expat for the past four years, I follow French pastry chefs on social media. I am often blown away by the photos they post on Instagram, each one more incredible than the last. I excitedly plan tastings whenever I return to France, but am frequently disappointed by the taste, which rarely lives up to my expectations and the promise conveyed by the pictures posted online. Rarely, until one day in May 2018.

AN EXTRAORDINARY ENCOUNTER!

François Perret's masterpiece–his Proustian madeleine–is testament to the mysterious magic of the art of patisserie. His trompe l'œil madeleine is a fusion of traditional and modern cuisine in a sublime wrapping. While the dessert looks exactly like a conventional madeleine, François Perret's genius becomes apparent when your silver fork divides the cake in two. Instead of finding simple sponge inside, you marvel at the slight tang of chestnut honey, the crunch of toasted almonds, the lightness of Savoy sponge, and the velvetiness of vanilla cream.

In 2018, I came across an article entitled, "François Perret's Stratospheric Patisseries." I read it, looked at the pictures, and soon developed an obsession with Perret's creations. I had to taste them, and soon. I took advantage of a business trip to Paris to visit the hotel where François Perret works, and I ordered all the desserts. The entire menu. Everything. The madeleine may have left its impact on Marcel Proust, but the feelings of nostalgia that its shell-like grooves evoke overwhelm all generations. Everyone has their own childhood reminiscences of this little cake in France, and each mouthful of Perret's entremets encapsulates a memory that will resonate inside you for a long time. His madeleine entremets, marble cake, vanilla meringue, caramel barquette, vanilla plated dessert, chocolate plated dessert, and . . . his iconic sugared strawberries with cream.

I'd like to take a moment to talk about this last dessert: sugared strawberries with cream.

Memories from my childhood come flooding back. The cool sea breeze that is carried all the way across the countryside and the scent of fresh herbs mingling under my nose create a fragrance that is forever anchored to my spirit. Whenever I went to visit my grandmother between April and September (the strawberry season), I eagerly awaited lunchtime for the real highlight of my visits: strawberries with sugar and cream. Has there ever been a dessert so simple yet so satisfying? I remember one sunny spring day, when I was devouring my strawberries, my grandmother took me aside to explain to me why it is scientifically necessary to add sugar to strawberries, even the best strawberries on earth. Was there a reason? The only reason in my eyes was because it was delicious! But in fact, as I discovered that day, the love of good food can converge with science. Sugar, when added to strawberries, produces a syrup. The fruit itself contains water and natural sugars, so adding sugar to the fruit triggers osmosis. The water, concentrated in the strawberry's juice, is drawn outward, giving it a sweeter, more syrupy taste and adding texture.

François's sugared strawberries could be ordinary-yet they are anything but.

A plate arrived at my table with several strawberries on it. The maître d'hôtel approached, added a spoonful of cream, and sprinkled large grains of sugar over the top. I looked at him, almost suspiciously. Was he pulling my leg? Was this really just strawberries with cream and sugar? I wondered if it was a joke. But, no, it wasn't. I picked up a strawberry with my spoon and put it in my mouth. The maître d' had told me to eat the green hull, so I did just that—and suddenly nothing was as it was supposed to be. Or rather, everything was even better.

As the strawberry exploded in my mouth, it was ecstasy. What was inside? It was impossible to describe. I cut the second strawberry to try and understand, and it was then that I realized the strawberries had been literally hollowed out. Only a thin layer of the outer flesh remained, and inside were succulent cooked and raw strawberries that had been finely chopped and macerated. They were accompanied by the finest cream from the French town of Bresse, a sprinkling of crunchy sugar, and a trompe l'œil hull that revealed itself to be a butter cookie flavored with basil.

The chocolate dessert arrived next. The maître d' informed me that this dish was not simply for tasting—I needed to use my other senses. All of my senses, I wondered? The plate was covered with a cloche and, before lifting it off, he told me to move closer, adding, "As soon as I remove the cloche, inhale deeply." I was intrigued, not only by what was hidden beneath the lid but also by what I was about to experience. The maître d' lifted the cloche, I took a deep breath, and everything around me reeled. The scent was indescribable: the aromas of chocolate were like nothing I'd ever smelled before, and the fragrance will be forever engraved on my memory.

The visual impact of the dessert followed, but, to be honest, I was a little disappointed after being hit with such an olfactory punch. There was a chocolate coil in the center, a *je ne sais quoi* that I could barely guess at, and chocolate sauce all around. The maître d' explained that the aroma was due to a chemical reaction between the very cold frozen parfait in the center of the chocolate coil and the hot serving plate. Inspired! With a preconceived idea of its texture, I got ready to taste this coiled chocolate serpent—and once again, my preconception was proven totally wrong. This chocolate serpent, whose visual impact fell short of the intensity of its aroma, was so designed to better deceive you and lead you in the wrong direction, as it was not a chocolate coil at all, but a butter cookie. The finest butter cookie that I have ever tasted, with an unimaginable flavor and texture. Who was the genius hiding behind these desserts?

There was only one thought in my head: I had to meet him.

MADELEINE ENTREMETS

I created a special mold myself to make this dessert. Here, however, I have adapted the recipe so that it can be made in a 5½-in. (14-cm) baking ring, with a depth of 2 in. (5 cm).

SERVES 4

PREPARATION: **3 HOURS + CHILLING AND FREEZING** ✳ COOKING: **38 MINUTES**
INFUSING: **10 MINUTES** ✳ LEVEL: **INTERMEDIATE**

INGREDIENTS

Savoy sponge cake with almonds
1 oz. (25 g) sliced almonds
2 medium eggs
  (scant ½ cup/100 g)
Scant ½ cup (3 oz./80 g) superfine
  sugar
1½ oz. (40 g) butter, melted and
  still warm
Generous ⅓ cup (1¾ oz./50 g)
  all-purpose flour
1 oz. (30 g) potato starch
¾ tsp baking powder
Butter and flour for the baking
  ring

Vanilla syrup
Scant ½ cup (100 ml) water
2½ tbsp (1 oz./30 g) superfine
  sugar
½ vanilla bean, split lengthwise

Caramel crémeux
1 sheet (2 g) gelatin
1 cup (12 oz./340 g) chestnut
  honey
Scant 2 tbsp (1½ oz./40 g) acacia
  honey
3 tbsp (60 g) glucose syrup
Scant 1 cup (210 ml) whipping
  cream
3 medium egg yolks (2¾ tbsp/45 g)

Pastry cream
½ vanilla bean, split lengthwise
Scant ⅔ cup (150 ml) whole milk
1 tsp unsalted butter
1 large egg yolk (1 tbsp/20 g)
2¼ tbsp (¾ oz./20 g) light brown
  sugar
1 tbsp (10 g) cornstarch

→

To prepare the sponge cake

Preheat the oven to 300°F (150°C/Gas Mark 2). Spread out the sliced almonds on a silicone baking mat or cookie sheet lined with parchment paper and toast them in the oven for about 8 minutes, watching them carefully to make sure they do not burn. Remove the almonds from the mat or sheet and set aside.

Increase the oven temperature to 325°F (160°C/Gas Mark 3) on fan setting.

Whisk the eggs and sugar together in a mixing bowl until pale and doubled in volume. Gently fold in the warm melted butter. Sift together the flour, potato starch, and baking powder, and fold into the whisked mixture using a flexible spatula.

Lightly grease the 4¾-in. (12-cm) baking ring with butter and dust with flour. Set the baking ring on the silicone mat or cookie sheet lined with fresh parchment paper. Pour the cake batter into the ring until it is half-filled, then scatter the toasted almonds over the top. Bake for 30 minutes.

Remove the cake from the oven and let cool. Unmold by running the blade of a knife around the edge, between the sponge and the ring, then lift off the ring. The sponge needs to be 1 in. (2.5 cm) thick, so trim the top using a serrated knife if necessary. Wash and dry the baking ring. Stretch plastic wrap over the top and set it upside down on the silicone mat or cookie sheet so the base is lined with the plastic wrap.

To prepare the vanilla syrup

Heat the water and sugar in a saucepan until the sugar dissolves. Bring to a boil and add the vanilla bean. Take off the heat and let infuse. When cool, lightly brush the syrup over the sponge to moisten it.

To prepare the caramel crémeux

Soak the gelatin in a bowl of cold water until softened. Heat the chestnut honey, acacia honey, and glucose in a saucepan until the temperature reaches 300°F (150°C) on an instant-read thermometer. While the honey mixture is heating, warm the cream in a separate saucepan. Stir the hot cream into the honey mixture to prevent further cooking. Remove from the heat.

→

Chantilly mousse
1 sheet (2 g) gelatin
1½ cups (350 ml) whipping cream
3½ oz. (100 g) pastry cream (see above)

Chocolate velvet mixture
4 oz. (110 g) dark chocolate, 70% cacao, chopped
1½ oz. (40 g) cacao paste
4½ oz. (125 g) cocoa butter, chopped

Gold velvet mixture
3½ oz. (100 g) white chocolate, chopped
⅓ oz. (10 g) milk chocolate, chopped
3½ oz. (100 g) cocoa butter, chopped
1½ tsp (8 g) edible gold luster dust

To serve
Honey

Equipment
Electric hand beater
4¾-in. (12-cm) baking ring
5½-in. (14-cm) baking ring
Instant-read thermometer
2 velvet spray guns

Set a mixing bowl over a bed of ice. Whisk the egg yolks in a separate bowl, then whisk in a little of the hot cream mixture. Pour it back into the saucepan and stir constantly over low heat until thickened. Do not let the custard boil; the surface must only ripple gently. As the quantity of custard is small, it will cook very quickly.

Squeeze out the gelatin to remove excess water and place it in the bowl set over ice. Immediately strain the hot custard through a fine-mesh sieve over the gelatin, stirring until the gelatin dissolves. Do not blend. Cool the custard quickly over the ice and pour it into the 4¾-in. (12-cm) baking ring to form a layer about ¾ in. (1.5 cm) deep. Any leftover crémeux can be poured into a jar and eaten later on bread.

When the caramel crémeux begins to set, place the sponge on top, with the almond side facing down. Keep chilled.

To prepare the pastry cream
Place the milk and butter in a saucepan and scrape in the vanilla seeds. Bring to a boil.

While the milk is heating, whisk the egg yolks and sugar together until pale and thick, then whisk in the cornstarch. Pour a little of the hot milk mixture into the egg yolks and sugar, whisking nonstop. Pour it back into the saucepan and cook over low heat, stirring constantly until thickened and smooth—it will cook very quickly. Pour onto a rimmed baking sheet lined with parchment paper and cool quickly.

To prepare the Chantilly mousse
Soak the gelatin in a bowl of cold water until softened. Drain and squeeze to remove excess water. Place in a bowl and microwave on full power for 5 seconds, or until melted.

Whip the cream in a mixing bowl until it holds soft peaks. Bring the pastry cream to room temperature and, using a flexible spatula, fold in the melted gelatin, then the whipped cream.

To prepare the chocolate and gold velvet mixtures
Place the ingredients for the velvet mixtures in two separate bowls and melt over pans of simmering water (bain-maries). Pass each one through a fine-mesh sieve and transfer to velvet spray guns. Use at a temperature of 113°F (45°C).

To assemble
Fit a 2-in. (5-cm) wide band of food-grade acetate around the inside of the 5½-in. (14-cm) baking ring. Unmold the sponge with the caramel crémeux and place it in the center of the ring, with the crémeux uppermost. Pour over the still-soft mousse. Freeze until well-chilled and firm, then remove the acetate band and baking ring. First, spray the gold velvet mixture all over the entremets. Spray the chocolate velvet mixture around the sides, then spray the top edges lightly to reflect the color of a baked madeleine. Finish off with a few drops of honey.

MY VANILLA CUSTARD

A simple, time-efficient recipe that gives instant pleasure!

<hr>

SERVES 4

<hr>

PREPARATION: **20 MINUTES** ✳ COOKING: **DEPENDS ON SAUCEPAN** ✳ RESTING: **OVERNIGHT** ✳ LEVEL: **EASY**

<hr>

Ingredients
5¼ cups (1.3 L) whole milk, divided
1 Bourbon vanilla bean
9 large egg yolks (¾ cup/160 g)
1 cup (5½ oz./160 g) light brown
  sugar
2 whole large eggs (½ cup/120 g)

Equipment
Immersion blender
Fine-mesh sieve
Electric hand beater
Instant-read thermometer

To infuse the milk

A day ahead, pour half the milk into a saucepan. Cut the vanilla bean into small pieces and add to the milk. Bring to a boil, then blend with an immersion blender.

Remove from the heat and add the rest of the milk. Cover and let cool. When cool, leave to infuse in the refrigerator overnight.

To prepare the custard

The next day, strain the milk through a fine-mesh sieve.

Whisk the egg yolks, sugar, and whole eggs together until pale, creamy, and thick.

Pour the infused milk into a saucepan and add the whisked eggs and sugar. Stir constantly over low heat using a spatula until the temperature reaches 180°F (82°C) on an instant-read thermometer. Make sure the custard does not boil; it should just simmer very gently.

As soon as the custard reaches the required temperature, immediately strain it through a fine-mesh sieve into a bowl. Press plastic wrap over the surface and cool it quickly, either by setting the bowl on a bed of ice or in the refrigerator, to prevent the custard from continuing to cook.

To serve

Serve the custard well chilled, with a slice of marble cake (see p. 24)—my very own Proustian madeleine!

MARBLE CAKE

You'll be surprised by just how light and airy this cake is. You can coat it with chocolate glaze, as I've done here, but it is even better straight from the oven, without being soaked in syrup or glazed. However, if you wish to store the cake, you will need to glaze it. This dessert is definitely one of my favorites, so enjoy!

MAKES 1 CAKE

PREPARATION: **1 HOUR** ✳ COOKING: **1½ HOURS** ✳ RESTING: **SEVERAL HOURS** ✳ LEVEL: **EASY**

INGREDIENTS

Vanilla cake batter
1 stick (4 oz./120 g) unsalted butter + extra for the pan
1½ cups (10½ oz./300 g) sugar
Scant 1 tsp (2 g) vanilla powder
Generous ¾ tsp (about 4 pinches) *fleur de sel* sea salt
2 large eggs (½ cup/120 g)
Scant 1¾ cups (7 oz./210 g) all-purpose flour
1½ tsp (6 g) baking powder
Generous ¾ cup (200 ml) whipping cream

Chocolate cake batter
½ cup (2 oz./60 g) unsweetened cocoa powder, sifted
1 tsp softened butter to pipe on the batters

Rum syrup
1 cup (250 ml) water
1 tbsp (15 ml) dark rum
2⅓ cups (1 lb./450 g) superfine sugar

Chocolate glaze
1 lb. 10 oz. (750 g) *pâte à glaçer brune* (brown glazing paste), chopped
9 oz. (250 g) dark chocolate, 70% cacao, chopped
½ cup (125 g) grape-seed oil

Equipment
Large loaf pan
Stand mixer or electric hand beater
2 pastry bags fitted with plain tips
Instant-read or candy thermometer
Immersion blender

To prepare the vanilla and chocolate cake batters

Grease a large loaf pan with butter. In the bowl of a stand mixer fitted with the whisk, beat the butter, sugar, vanilla powder, and salt until light and creamy. Add the eggs and whisk in. Scrape down the sides of the bowl using a dough scraper, sift in the flour and baking powder, and incorporate on low speed. Immediately pour in the cream and whisk again until the batter is smooth.

Spoon slightly less than half the batter into a separate bowl. Stir in the cocoa powder to make the chocolate batter.

Preheat the oven to 300°F (150°C/Gas Mark 2).

Transfer the vanilla and chocolate cake batters to two separate pastry bags, each fitted with large plain tips. Pipe the batters alternately into the loaf pan.

Spoon the softened butter into a paper piping cone, snip off the tip, and pipe a line of butter lengthwise down the center of the batter.

Bake for about 1½ hours, watching it carefully: the cake is ready when the tip of a knife pushed into the center comes out clean.

To prepare the syrup

Heat the water, rum, and sugar in a saucepan, stirring until the sugar dissolves. Bring to a boil and set aside.

Remove the cake from the oven and immediately turn it out onto a wire rack. Brush the syrup over it. Cover the cake with plastic wrap while it is still hot. Let cool, then refrigerate for several hours until ready to glaze.

To glaze the cake

Melt the glaze ingredients together in a bowl over a pan of simmering water (bain-marie), until the temperature reaches 113°F (45°C) on an instant-read thermometer. Blend with an immersion blender until smooth, strain through a fine-mesh sieve, and pour over the chilled cake.

SUGARED STRAWBERRIES WITH CREAM

This is the recipe that left Éric awestruck.

SERVES 8

PREPARATION: **1½ HOURS** ✳ RESTING: **1 HOUR** ✳ COOKING: **35 MINUTES** ✳ LEVEL: **INTERMEDIATE**

INGREDIENTS

Strawberry juice
2 lb. (1 kg) strawberries for making jams
¼ cup (1¾ oz./50 g) superfine sugar

Strawberry filling
2 sheets (5 g) gelatin
5½ oz. (150 g) strawberry jam
3½ oz. (100 g) strawberries (reserved from preparing the juice), diced
48–56 large strawberries, depending on size

Basil-flavored *langue de chats* batter
¼ oz. (5 g) fresh basil leaves
6 tbsp (3 oz./85 g) butter, softened
¾ cup (3½ oz./100 g) confectioners' sugar, sifted
Scant ½ cup (3½ oz./105 g) egg whites, at room temperature
1 pinch salt
Generous ¾ cup (3½ oz./100 g) all-purpose flour, sifted
Green food coloring

Strawberry glaze
1⅓ cups (315 ml) strawberry juice (see above)
2 tbsp (30 ml) water
1 tbsp (12 g) superfine sugar
1½ tsp (6 g) pectin NH

To assemble
1 carton of whipping or heavy cream
Light brown sugar

→

To prepare the strawberry juice
Place the strawberries and sugar in a heatproof bowl and cover with plastic wrap. Place over a pan of simmering water (bain-marie) for 1 hour. Strain through a fine-mesh sieve and reserve the juice. Set aside the strawberries for the strawberry filling.

To prepare the strawberry filling
Soak the gelatin in a bowl of cold water until softened. Drain and squeeze to remove excess water. Place in a bowl and microwave on full power for 5 seconds, or until melted. Place the strawberry jam in a large bowl. Dice 3½ oz. (100 g) of the strawberries reserved from making the juice and fold them into the jam, along with the melted gelatin. Hull and hollow out each large strawberry. Trim a thin slice from the side of each one to sit them at a slight angle on the serving plate. Fill with the strawberry filling and place in the silicone mold half-sphere cavities so they remain upright until the gelatin sets (about 1 hour).

To prepare the basil-flavored *langue de chats* batter
Preheat the oven to 95°F (35°C/gas on the lowest setting). Spread out the basil leaves on a silicone baking mat or lined baking sheet and dry them out in the oven for about 25 minutes, or until they can be crumbled easily. Grind to a fine powder.
  Whisk the butter until smooth, then whisk in the confectioners' sugar. Whisk in the egg whites and salt, followed by the sifted flour and powdered basil. Color the batter with a little green food coloring. Transfer to a covered container until needed.
  Preheat the oven to 340°F (170°C/Gas Mark 3) on fan setting. Lay the stencil on a silicone baking mat and spread a little of the batter over it using a spatula. Repeat with the remaining batter. Bake for about 10 minutes. Remove from the oven and immediately lay each one carefully in a half-sphere cavity in the silicone mold, or in a teaspoon, so that they cool in a curved shape.

To prepare the strawberry glaze
Heat the strawberry juice with the water. Carefully mix the sugar and pectin together well. When the temperature of the juice reaches 140°F (60°C), add the sugar and pectin and stir in until

→

Equipment
Electric hand beater
Instant-read thermometer
Silicone mold with half-sphere
  cavities measuring 1½ in. (4 cm)
  in diameter
Cardboard stencil in the shape of
  the hull of a strawberry
Toothpicks

incorporated. Simmer for 1–2 minutes. Transfer to a covered container. When ready to use, reheat the glaze gently in the microwave—it must not boil. Use the glaze melted but cold.

To assemble

Whip the cream until it forms soft peaks. Sift the light brown sugar, keeping only the largest grains. Using toothpicks, prick the strawberries all over (leave one in to transfer to the serving plate). Coat in a thin, even layer of glaze. Arrange 6 or 7 in a ring on each serving plate, with the tips pointing inward. Leave room in the center to add a large spoonful of whipped cream. Remove the toothpicks and carefully place a *langue de chat* hull on the top of each strawberry. Sprinkle with the sugar and serve immediately.

MILK BRIOCHE CLOUD WITH CARAMEL SAUCE

SERVES 4

PREPARATION: **1 HOUR** ✳ RESTING: **OVERNIGHT** ✳ COOKING: **15 MINUTES** ✳ LEVEL: **EASY**

INGREDIENTS

Brioche inserts
1 large mousseline brioche (with as compact a crumb as possible)

Milk for soaking
1 sheet gelatin
Scant 1½ cups (350 ml) whole milk, divided
5 tsp (20 g) superfine sugar
1 vanilla bean, split lengthwise
⅓ cup (80 ml) whipping cream

Blancmange
1 sheet gelatin
3 large egg whites (½ cup/90 g)
⅓ cup (2½ oz./70 g) superfine sugar

Caramel sauce
Scant ⅓ cup (70 ml) whipping cream
1 vanilla bean, split lengthwise
Scant ½ cup (3 oz./90 g) superfine sugar
½ stick (1¾ oz./50 g) lightly salted butter, diced

To serve
Sliced almonds

Equipment
1⅓-in. (3.5-cm) round cookie cutter
Instant-read or candy thermometer
Immersion blender
4 × 3-in. (8-cm) baking rings, 1½ in. (4 cm) deep

To prepare the brioche inserts
A day ahead, cut 4 × 1⅓-in. (3.5-cm) thick slices of brioche using a serrated knife. Using the cookie cutter, cut out 1⅓-in. (3.5-cm) cylinders from the center of each slice. Keep the trimmings for breakfast or for breadcrumbs.

To prepare the milk for soaking
Soak the gelatin in a bowl of cold water until softened. Drain and squeeze to remove excess water. Place in a bowl and microwave on full power for 5 seconds, or until melted.

Place half of the milk, the sugar, and the vanilla bean and scraped-out seeds in a saucepan and heat until the temperature reaches 122°F (50°C). Add the melted gelatin, then pour in the rest of the milk and the cream.

Pour the mixture into a dish large enough to accommodate the brioche inserts in a single layer. Let them soak for a minimum of 2 hours, turning them over every 20 minutes.

Once the brioche inserts are thoroughly soaked, place them in a covered container and chill until ready to assemble the dish the next day.

To prepare the blancmange
The next day, soak the gelatin in a bowl of cold water until softened.

Whisk the egg whites until they form soft peaks, then gradually whisk in the sugar, without letting the egg whites become too stiff. Drain the gelatin and squeeze to remove excess water. Place in a bowl and microwave on full power for 5 seconds, or until melted and hot. Add to the egg whites, then stop whisking. Set aside.

To prepare the caramel sauce
Heat the cream to a simmer with the vanilla bean and scraped-out seeds.

In a separate saucepan, prepare a dry caramel by heating the sugar in a heavy-based saucepan without adding water. Once the sugar dissolves to form a syrup, boil it until it becomes a light golden-brown caramel and the temperature reaches a maximum of 340°F (170°C).

→

Take the pan off the heat and very carefully pour in the hot cream. Add the butter and blend with an immersion blender until smooth. Strain through a fine-mesh sieve. Set aside.

To assemble

Preheat the oven to 525°F (280°C, or its highest setting). Place the baking rings on a silicone baking mat or cookie sheet lined with lightly oiled parchment paper. Spread a layer of blancmange around the insides of the rings. Place a milk-soaked brioche insert in the center, with its base touching the mat or cookie sheet. Cover with more blancmange and smooth the surface. Run a knife around the inside of the ring, then carefully remove it. If desired, you can sprinkle sliced almonds over the top of the blancmange.

Place in the hot oven and immediately switch it off. Let cook for 10 minutes in the turned-off oven. This is to cook, stiffen up, and keep the blancmange airy, without coloring it.

Remove from the oven and let cool. Keep chilled.

To serve

Serve the brioche clouds well chilled. Spoon the caramel sauce over them at the table, in front of your guests, making sure it runs invitingly down the sides. However, avoid adding too much sauce to ensure they are not excessively sweet.

BUDDHA'S-HAND PAVLOVA WITH CREAMY RICE PUDDING AND CRISPY MERINGUE

This dessert is very light and airy yet extremely voluminous. The concept was to produce maximum volume with the minimum of weight. Equally astonishing is the fruit used to make this dessert, which looks straight out of a Japanese anime. Its subtle and delicate fragrance cannot fail to seduce.

SERVES 4

PREPARATION: **3 HOURS** ✳ COOKING: **1½ HOURS** ✳ LEVEL: **INTERMEDIATE**

INGREDIENTS

Meringue
6 large egg whites (generous ¾ cup/190 g)
1 scant cup (6 oz./170 g) superfine sugar
1⅓ cups (6 oz./170 g) confectioners' sugar, sifted

Buddha's-hand ribbons
1 Buddha's-hand
2 cups (450 ml) water
¾ cup (5 oz./150 g) superfine sugar

Diced Buddha's-hand "fingers"
"Fingers" from the Buddha's-hand used for the ribbons
Reserved hot syrup from the ribbons (see above)

Buddha's-hand sauce
Generous ½ cup (130 ml) remaining syrup from poaching the ribbons and "fingers"
3 tbsp (50 ml) water
¼ vanilla bean, split lengthwise and seeds scraped
4 tsp (20 ml) lemon juice
1½ tsp (5 g) potato starch

→

To prepare the meringue
Preheat the oven to 180°F (80°C/gas on lowest setting). Whisk the egg whites until they form soft peaks, then gradually whisk in the superfine sugar until the peaks are firm. Gently fold in the confectioners' sugar using a spatula until incorporated.

Transfer the meringue to the pastry bag fitted with a sultan tip and pipe 16–20 mounds onto a silicone baking mat or cookie sheet lined with parchment paper. Bake for 1½ hours. Let cool on a wire rack.

To prepare the Buddha's-hand ribbons
Clean the Buddha's-hand fruit thoroughly using a toothbrush. Cut the "palm" of the fruit into very thin ribbons using a food slicer or mandoline. Reserve the "fingers" for the sorbet.

Bring the sugar and water to a boil in a saucepan, stirring to dissolve the sugar. Continue to boil until the syrup reaches a temperature of 158°F (70°C). Maintain the syrup at this temperature.

Blanch the ribbons in a saucepan of boiling water for 1 minute. Drain, then plunge them immediately into the hot syrup. Cover with plastic wrap and let cool to room temperature. Drain, reserving the syrup for the "fingers."

To prepare the diced Buddha's-hand "fingers"
Dice the reserved Buddha's-hand "fingers." Reheat the reserved syrup used for the ribbons to 158°F (70°C). Blanch and drain the diced "fingers," then immerse them immediately in the hot syrup. Cover with plastic wrap and let cool to room temperature. Set aside 5¾ oz. (160 g) of the diced "fingers" for the sorbet. Reserve the rest to assemble the dessert.

To prepare the Buddha's-hand sauce
Heat a generous ½ cup (130 ml) of the syrup used to poach the ribbons and "fingers" with the water, lemon juice, and vanilla bean and seeds. Whisk in the potato starch until combined.

→

Creamy rice pudding
Generous ¾ cup (6 oz./170 g) short-grain rice
4 cups (1 L) whole milk
Generous ⅓ cup (2¾ oz./75 g) superfine sugar
2 vanilla beans, split lengthwise and seeds scraped
Generous ½ cup (150 ml) whipping cream

Buddha's-hand sorbet
1 cup (260 ml) whole milk
1 cup (260 ml) water
Scant ½ cup (3 oz./80 g) superfine sugar
5¾ oz. (160 g) diced Buddha's-hand "fingers" poached in syrup (see above)

To serve
1 finger lime
Lemon basil cress
1 lemon

Equipment
Pastry bag fitted with a sultan tip (see Chef's Notes)
Food slicer or mandoline
Instant-read thermometer
Pastry bag fitted with a large plain tip
Thermomix or spice grinder (or blender)
Ice-cream maker (see Chef's Notes)

Cook for a few minutes until the sauce has slightly thickened. Watch over it closely as it cooks very quickly. Strain through a fine-mesh sieve and set aside.

To prepare the creamy rice pudding
Blanch the rice in a saucepan of boiling water for 8 minutes. Drain and rinse the rice thoroughly with cold water.

Place the milk, sugar, blanched rice, and vanilla bean and scraped-out seeds in a saucepan. Cook over low heat for 50 minutes, stirring regularly, then turn the heat down to its lowest setting and cook for an additional 20 minutes. Let cool completely.

Whip the cream in a mixing bowl until it holds soft peaks. Once the rice has cooled, fold in the whipped cream and spoon into the pastry bag fitted with a large plain tip.

To prepare the Buddha's-hand sorbet
Make a syrup by heating the milk, water, and sugar until the sugar dissolves. Bring to a boil, remove from the heat, and let cool.

Blend the diced Buddha's-hand with the cooled syrup in the Thermomix or spice grinder (or blender). Pour into the bowl of an ice-cream maker and churn according to the manufacturer's instructions. If you do not have an ice-cream maker, transfer the mixture to ice-cube bags and freeze; when frozen, place in the Thermomix (or blender) and blend briefly to obtain a sorbet. Store in a covered container in the freezer until using.

To assemble
Place 4 or 5 meringues in the center of each serving plate. Pipe creamy rice pudding into the hollow in the middle of each one and add the remaining diced Buddha's-hand set aside earlier.

Top each meringue with 3 small quenelles of Buddha's-hand sorbet and the Buddha's-hand ribbons rolled into curls, allowing 12 curls per serving. Scrape out the beads of "caviar" from the finger lime. Place a little on each pavlova, along with a few tiny sprigs of lemon basil cress. Grate over a little lemon zest at the table, in front of your guests, and pour a little of the sauce over each serving.

Chef's Notes
• A sultan piping tip is a large tip with a fluted edge and hollow center for piping fluted rings.
• If you do not have an ice-cream maker, buy a good-quality lemon sorbet.

Living over 6,000 miles away, I set François a challenge: to leave his 5-star hotel kitchen to drive around Los Angeles in a food truck. The aim: to taste all the classic dishes that the City of Angels has to offer and reinterpret them for passersby in Downtown LA to taste his take on tacos, donuts, and cookies! François accepted, bade *au revoir* to his team, and was off. Destination: Los Angeles!

CALIFORNIA

The sights and sounds of the City of Angels are endlessly fascinating. All we were missing now were the smells and tastes, and I knew just the place to complete the Californian experience. First stop was Teddy's Red Tacos. Los Angeles's taco culture is almost as old as the city itself, and the taco is to Los Angeles what cheesecake is to Philadelphia.

It all began in the 1880s, during the city's Wild West era, when horse-drawn tamale wagons from Mexico descended on the town en masse. As successive waves of immigrants arrived throughout the twentieth century, these taco trucks took on an important role: they became the melting pot that brought together Los Angeles's many different cultures, and street food was born. Tacos were discovered by Angelinos, who appreciated them for their simplicity, their new and incredibly rich flavors, and their short preparation time, allowing customers to order a hot meal and take it away with them.

Many of these migrants came to Los Angeles—and still come today—in search of a better life. The food truck and its horse-drawn predecessor have become symbols of the American dream for migrants, who, with few means and thanks to word of mouth and incredibly flavorful cuisine, were able to create prosperous businesses, bypassing the racist and culturally discriminatory laws in place at the time that prohibited non-whites from running restaurants from established premises. As a result, the food truck became, and remains today, a path to freedom, where the only thing that seems important for success is how much love is put into the food.

Since the nineteenth century, various governments have attempted in vain to regulate or even restrict the number of food trucks in LA, but their popularity among residents has only grown over time.

Today, food trucks are a must-see attraction for any visitor to the City of Angels. Teddy's Red Tacos is the perfect illustration of the diversity of Mexican-Californian fusion food. Teddy's secret recipe (which he did not want to share with us for this book!) is made from beef that is slowly simmered in a rich tomato-based ragout, known as *birria*, until the meat is so tender it almost melts. Unsurprisingly, *birria* means "a delicious savory dish, full of culture and tradition." This method of preparing tacos has its roots in the Mexican state of Jalisco, where goat meat was originally used for the ragout. Goats, brought by the conquistadors in the sixteenth century, were at first considered a nuisance both for the crops and the soil. They reproduced too quickly and ate such a large part of the harvest that they indirectly caused a famine. During this famine, goats began to be used for their meat, despite the pronounced flavor and smell. To overcome this problem, different herbs and spices were added. Teddy's tacos—authentic beef *birriero*—are filled with onion, cilantro, and a spicy sauce, combining the best of the traditional recipe with a marvelously fresh, original (and red!) twist. It is the stuff that dreams are made of.

Éric: "What did you think? You can't find that in Paris, huh?"

François: "No, no, no. You know, I'm not a fan of spicy food, so it didn't make for a very easy start to this adventure, but besides the spices, I must say that it really wasn't bad at all! And it really helped me to project in terms of the next phase of this adventure. Seeing them work like that in the truck . . . in such a cramped space—but also seeing the concept of his recipe—gave me the idea of using the brioche dough on a plancha for my dessert version of the taco."

MILK JAR COOKIES

In our quest to discover what patisserie means to Americans, the different stops we made on this leg of our adventure were the cornerstone of our mission: enter cookies, donuts, and ice cream.

Our first stop was Milk Jar Cookies in the district of Beverly Hills. American cookies are much larger and deeper than French cookies. However, even if our two versions differ, we still eat them in the same way, by dunking them in milk—which is a must! The apparently worldwide ritual triggers an immediate wave of nostalgia, as this comforting touch transports us directly back to our childhood.

Although history tells us that cookies appeared in Persia during the seventh century, it was the Dutch who brought them to America toward the end of the 1620s. They only became popular in their modern incarnation (a creamy mixture of butter and sugar) during the eighteenth century. The most famous American cookie, the chocolate chip, was invented during the Great Depression by Ruth Wakefield, who broke up pieces of chocolate and added them to her cookie dough. It rapidly became very popular with Americans, and when the cookies were later sent overseas to American troops stationed abroad, their popularity spread worldwide. Today, chocolate chip cookies are without doubt the most famous cookie in the world.

At Milk Jar Cookies, innovation is the name of the game. In addition to the birthday cookie (a sugar cookie rolled in rainbow sprinkles), their other flavors include oatmeal chocolate chip, chocolate peanut butter, chocolate pecan caramel, and white chocolate with raspberries. Their method of baking most of their cookies differs slightly from that in France, as they preheat a conventional oven to 300°F (150°C/Gas Mark 2) and then lower the temperature to 275°F (140°C/Gas Mark 1) when the cookies go into the oven. In France, cookies are usually baked at a higher temperature. (The cookie recipe on p. 60 reflects the French method.)

At Milk Jar Cookies, innovation is the name of the game. In addition to the birthday cookie (a sugar cookie rolled in rainbow sprinkles), their other flavors include oatmeal chocolate chip, chocolate peanut butter, chocolate pecan caramel, and white chocolate with raspberries.

CHOCOLATE PECAN AND CARAMEL COOKIES

BY COURTNEY COWAN

MAKES 15–18 LARGE COOKIES (ABOUT 3 IN./8 CM IN DIAMETER)

PREPARATION: **25 MINUTES** ✳ COOKING: **12–14 MINUTES PER BATCH** ✳ STORAGE: **UP TO 4 DAYS IN AN AIRTIGHT CONTAINER OR 1 MONTH IN THE FREEZER (UNBAKED DOUGH)** ✳ LEVEL: **EASY**

INGREDIENTS

3½ cups (15½ oz./430 g)
  all-purpose flour
⅓ cup (1⅓ oz./40 g) unsweetened
  cocoa powder
1 tsp baking soda
1 tsp salt
1¼ sticks + 1 tbsp (5½ oz./160 g)
  unsalted butter, well chilled and
  diced
⅔ cup (4½ oz./125 g) shortening
  (white vegetable fat), at room
  temperature and diced
1 cup (6¾ oz./190 g) sugar
1 generous cup (7¾ oz./220 g)
  light brown sugar
2 extra-large eggs (½ cup/130 g)
1½ tsp vanilla extract
1½ cups (6½ oz./180 g) pecan
  pieces
30–36 Rolo caramel candies,
  halved (4 halves per cookie,
  approximately 72 halves)

Equipment
Stand mixer fitted with the paddle
  beater

To prepare the cookie dough

Preheat the oven to 350°F (180°C/Gas Mark 4).

Sift the flour, cocoa powder, baking soda, and salt into a mixing bowl. Set aside.

Combine the butter, shortening, sugars, eggs, and vanilla extract in the bowl of a stand mixer fitted with the paddle beater. Beat on medium-low speed for about 30 seconds, until the ingredients are combined but there are still small chunks of butter remaining. Each time the ingredients are mixed, scrape down the sides of the bowl with a spatula to be sure all the ingredients are incorporated—every bit matters!

Add half of the dry ingredients and mix on low speed until just incorporated and no flour is visible (about 30 seconds).

Add half of the remaining dry ingredients and mix on low speed until the flour is incorporated and there are no more chunks of butter (about 20 seconds).

Add the remaining dry ingredients and mix until the dough pulls away from the sides of the bowl and is no longer sticky to the touch (another 20 seconds). Be careful not to overmix, as that can result in flat cookies. Mix in the pecan pieces.

To bake the cookies

Line 2 cookie sheets with parchment paper.

Scoop up ⅓ cup (3 oz./80 g) of the dough at a time, place 2 Rolo halves in the center of each one, and firmly roll into balls measuring approximately 1½ in. (3 cm) in diameter. With a ball in your hand, top with 2 more Rolo halves, gently pushing them in to keep them in position while they bake. Place 6 balls of dough on each cookie sheet, spacing them well apart.

Place the sheets in the oven on the middle and lower racks and bake for approximately 12–14 minutes, or until the caramel candies are melted and hairline cracks start appearing around the sides of the cookies. Turn each cookie sheet 180 degrees and swap their positions on the racks halfway through the cooking time.

Let the cookies cool on the sheets for 10 minutes, then use a wide spatula to transfer them to a wire rack or sheet of parchment paper on the worktop, to cool completely. Let the cookie sheets cool before repeating with the remaining balls of cookie dough.

AMERICAN DESSERTS

Desserts stateside have been strongly influenced by the flavors of Northern Europe (mainly German and Dutch), which immigrants from that region brought over with them. Their recipes spread throughout a large part of the eastern United States.

This is one of the reasons why the typically American, famously supersized cakes are found in this part of the country. I really wanted François to discover these giants of the pastry world, so we set ourselves up in our test kitchen and prepared a customized tasting for him: American apple pie (one with a puff pastry crust, and another with shortcrust pastry, which retains more moisture than a French-style *tarte Tatin*), blueberry pie, mixed-berry pie, carrot cake, red velvet cake, and cereal pie, among others. Visually impressive, they remain loyal to American tradition. American pies are covered with another layer of pastry, unlike open-faced French tarts, so the fruit is steamed beneath it, becoming caramelized and even more delectable.

Éric: "I can officially say that I lived my childhood dream today: I spent the entire day eating dessert!"

François: "I can't argue with you there! You definitely have a sweet tooth, and these cakes, well, the least I can say is that they're—what's the word? Generous!"

Éric: "Oh, come on! The carrot cake was incredible!"

François: "Incredibly . . . sweet?"

Éric: "Seriously? I loved it!"

François: "I get it, but Éric, all these cakes look very much alike. When you think about it a little, it really is just sponge cake and cream cheese . . . that they add flavor to according to the color!"

Éric: "That's true. Except perhaps for the carrot cake? The marvelous texture of the pecans, the finely grated carrots, and those small explosions of cinnamon and raisins! That's what I call a dessert!"

François: "Yes, maybe the carrot cake, but it remains very simple! Don't you see? Here, in the United States, cakes are all made the same way: by alternating layers of sponge cake and buttercream, which is then all covered in cream-cheese icing. A very basic structure, which, historically, was easier, faster, and less expensive to make, especially at the time of the first frontier settlers. In France, our cakes are all different from one another. A mille-feuille is different from a macaron. We are talking about two cakes whose textures and recipes have nothing in common, and they taste radically different. Our cakes result from a long tradition of great pastry chefs who considered pastry-making as an art form. We experiment a bit like chemists do in a lab. We never stop creating."

DONUTS

We stopped off next to try another iconic American pastry: the donut. Unlike European versions, the classic American donut is extremely sweet and usually made from deep-fried dough filled with pastry cream around the outer edge, with a hole in the middle.

The donut follows a historical path similar to that of the cookie. Donuts were originally a Dutch specialty, known as *oliekoek*, imported by Dutch settlers into New Amsterdam (modern-day New York) and American culture in the seventeenth century. Originally, they were simply balls of sweet dough deep-fried in fat, without the characteristic hole in the middle that distinguishes them today. In the mid-nineteenth century, the donut acquired its modern shape and became a classic American pastry.

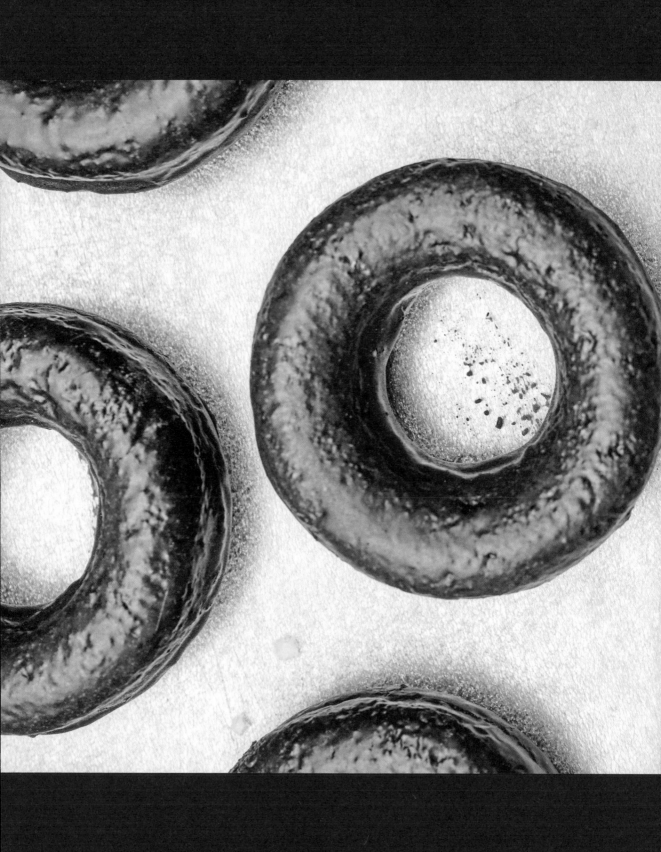

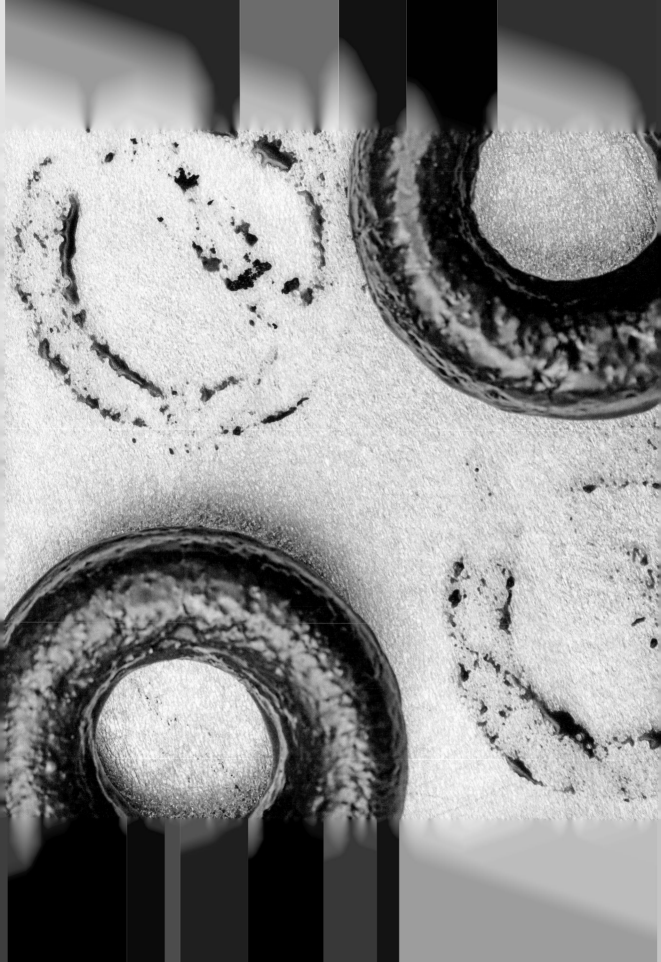

CHEZ ROSE

Finally, we headed to The Rose restaurant in Venice, where the chef showed us his own Buddha's-hand creation. This is a savory version, in which the Buddha's-hand is preserved in olive oil with a touch of sugar, set on a plate of asparagus with dehydrated pesto and yuzu. And to follow, agnolotti to die for! Extraordinary.

Next, François tried his hand at making a dessert taco based on asparagus, with hazelnut praline, filled with a Meyer lemon yogurt sauce and topped with Parmesan and yuzu ponzu sauce. Who would have thought that vegetables could make such good desserts?

François: "The return of the Buddha's-hand! What an unexpected twist!"

Éric: "It was a marvelous meal, don't you think?"

François: "It was marvelous to see the same passion here as in our kitchens in Paris. It's all about making your customers happy and providing them with the best experience possible. It's like what Chef Jason said: 'That's what dining is. It's communion. It's to commune with one another. In this day and age, where people are constantly in front of their screens, it's a time to share and be together. It's a universal language. Let's look at each other and share, enjoy, talk—let's fight over that last piece of pasta.'"

Éric: "We really did fight over that last piece of pasta, didn't we?"

François: "How could we not have, with that agnolotti? I promise you that I am going to make it at home if Jason is kind enough to give me the recipe."

SWEET CORN AGNOLOTTI

BY JASON NERONI AT THE ROSE VENICE

SERVES 4

PREPARATION: **30 MINUTES** ✶ RESTING: **30 MINUTES** ✶ COOKING: **2 MINUTES** ✶ LEVEL: **EASY**

INGREDIENTS

Sweet corn purée
4 corn cobs
2 sticks (8 oz./230 g) brown butter
Brown sugar, if needed
Salt

Pasta dough
1 lb. 6 oz. (625 g) Caputo flour
  (see Chef's Notes)
1½ cups (300 g) egg yolks
Scant ½ cup (100 ml) water

To serve
1 tbsp butter
3 tbsp roasted corn kernels
1 tsp lemon juice
1 tbsp Cotija cheese (see Chef's
  Notes)
Sprigs of micro cilantro
Ground tajine spices

Equipment
Immersion blender
Pastry bag fitted with a plain tip
Stand mixer fitted with the dough
  hook
Brass pasta wheel or ravioli rolling
  cutter

To prepare the sweet corn purée

Blanch the corn cobs until they are tender. Drain and, using a sharp knife, cut the kernels off the cobs. Using an immersion blender, blend the kernels with the brown butter to make a very smooth purée. Add brown sugar and salt to taste. Let the purée cool, then transfer it to the pastry bag fitted with a plain tip.

To prepare the pasta dough and make the agnolotti

Place the flour in the bowl of a stand mixer fitted with the dough hook. Add the egg yolks, then gradually add the water, until the ingredients are evenly combined. Knead for about 10 minutes. Shape the dough into a ball, cover in plastic wrap, and let rest for 30 minutes.

Once the dough has rested, roll it into a long, very thin sheet.

Pipe the sweet corn purée in a line down one side of the sheet, dampen the edge of the dough with water, and fold it over to enclose the filling. Using a brass pasta wheel or ravioli rolling cutter, cut the pasta crosswise into short lengths to make agnolotti.

To cook and serve the agnolotti

Bring a large pan of salted water to a boil. Add the agnolotti and boil for about 2 minutes, until they float. Drain the agnolotti, reserving a little of the cooking water.

Melt the butter with a splash of the reserved cooking water in a large skillet. Add the roasted corn and lemon juice, then mix in the agnolotti.

Divide between 4 serving dishes and crumble over the Cotija cheese. Garnish with sprigs of micro cilantro and a dusting of ground tajine spices.

Chef's Notes

• Caputo 00 flour is a high-quality wheat flour from Naples. Very finely ground, it is used for making both pasta and pizza doughs.
• Cotija is a Mexican cheese made from cow's milk. When dried, it can be grated like Parmesan. In this recipe, however, the fresher version is used and is crumbled over the agnolotti. If it is unavailable, feta can be substituted.

HEAVENLY ICE CREAM

After this fabulous meal, we needed something refreshing to aid our digestion, and what better than an ice cream from Salt & Straw? This artisan ice cream store combines incredible flavors, such as salted ice cream with hand-burned caramel, almond brittle, honey lavender, and black olive and goat cheese.

Éric: "What's your verdict on the olive and goat cheese ice cream?"

François: "Hard to say."

Éric: "You don't like the combination of sweet and savory?"

François: "Of course I do! I just made asparagus and praline tacos at The Rose! I make fennel desserts; I mix black truffle with chocolate. It's not that at all. I just don't think that the flavor of the ice cream works. At the same time, you tricked me. I should have ordered what you got: it was amazing! Salted ice cream with ribbons of butterscotch! Next time, I won't take your advice."

REINVENTING

After all these tastings, it was finally time to think about our own reinterpretations and start hunting down ingredients. In Paris, François was used to having local producers come to the hotel with superior quality produce, but here it was a whole new challenge to find the best ingredients.
So we began with a hands-on adventure, to say the least—at a dairy farm, where we tried milking cows. There's definitely a skill to it.

We continued on to The Valley Hive: an enormous honey farm, where the hives were fascinating and buzzing with activity. We discovered an interesting bit of trivia: one side of a hive is much warmer than the other because the bees are sitting on their babies and must keep the air at room temperature. After a brief tour of the beekeeping facilities, we finally moved on to the sweeter part: tasting the honey. The unique flavors included sage honey, buckwheat honey, and avocado honey. Each variety was a delicious combination of sweetness and bitterness.

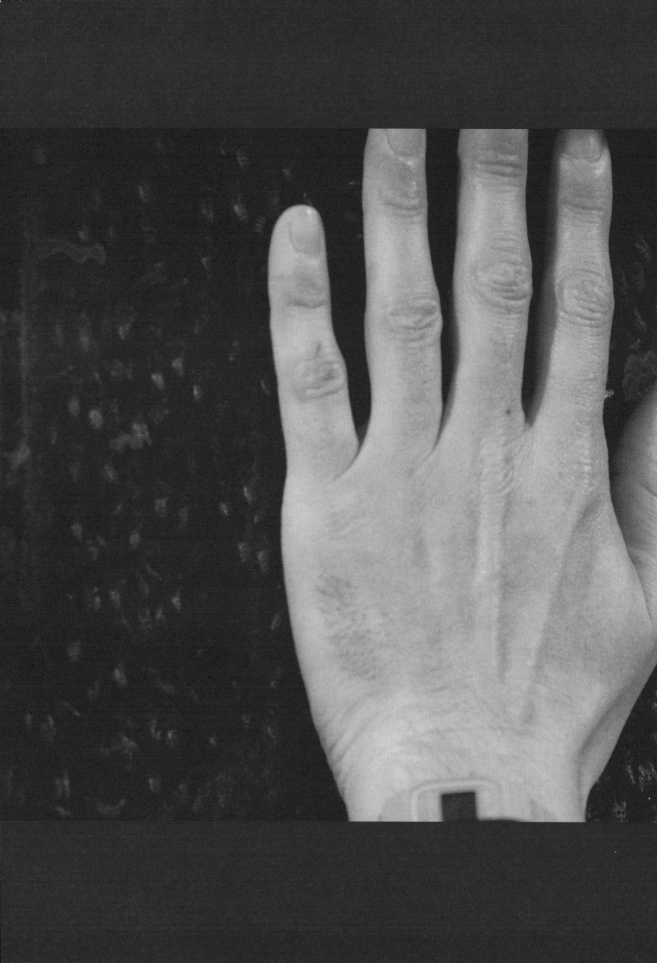

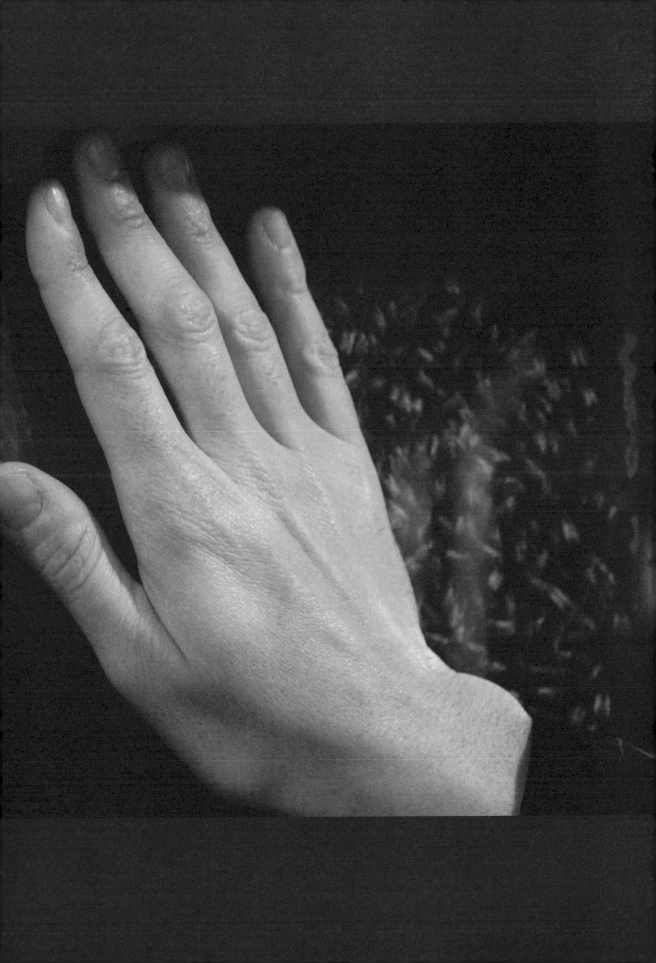

François: "I have to say, Éric. I'm feeling inspired. This honey—I'm really taken by its flavors. In France, I've visited many beekeepers, and I must say that I see the same passion here."

Éric: "We have time to experiment. Let's go see what our truck can do!"

Before heading to the next producer, it was time to experiment a little: a waffle dough for the honey tacos, similar to an ice-cream sandwich that we saw at Milk Jar Cookies.

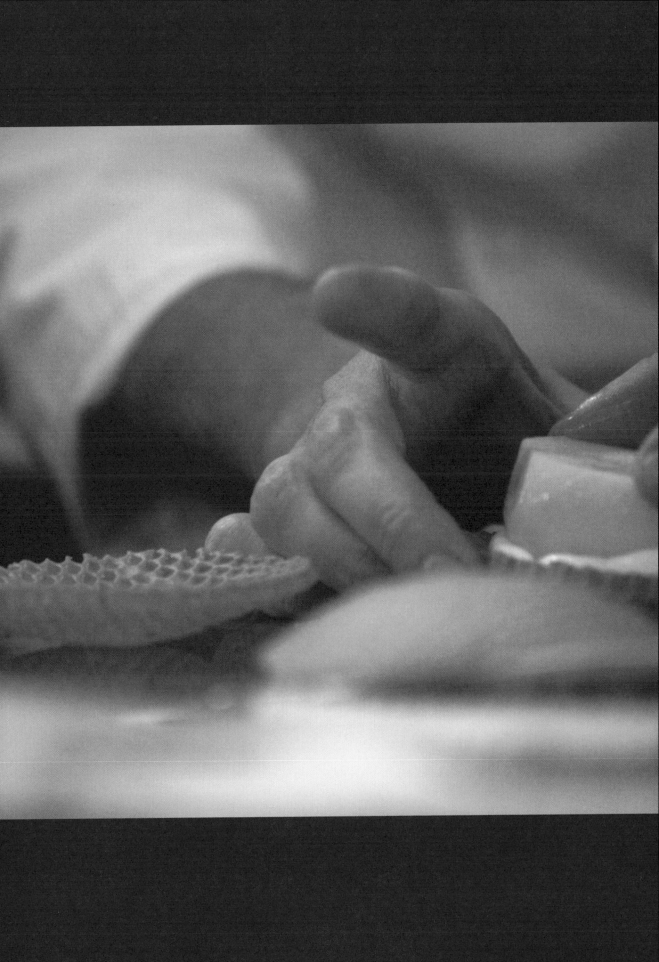

Speaking of cookies, it was time to think about how we would reinterpret them. Pistachio cookies, perhaps. We headed to a pistachio orchard to taste the produce and see how large-scale American growers manage the production process and harvests.

The pistachio orchard was still dormant, but the trees were about to blossom. Pistachios rely on the wind for pollination, with the pollen coming from the male trees. When the nuts are harvested in September, the shells are already open; every variety has its own shape and, in some cases, taste. François also discovered many Buddha's-hands growing on a Californian tree!

FARMERS' MARKET

When we arrived at the farmers' market recommended to us by Michelin-starred chef Niki Nakayama, we realized we'd made the mistake of arriving too late. As a result, there was very little produce left. Still, our spirits lifted when we found a small stall with kumquats the size of lemons, as well as the best avocados in the world. Instantly, they inspired François, who pictured a dessert made from kumquats and avocado, in the shape of a giant kumquat filled with avocado ice cream that you could bite into. It sounded heavenly!

On the way back to the food truck, there was a little drama when the bag containing the avocados and kumquats was lost. Of course, there is nothing more frustrating than envisaging a creation but being denied the means to carry it out and give others pleasure. But, hey, the show must go on. It seemed a minor setback for everyone else, but for François—who had a particular idea in mind, a dream he wanted to turn into a reality—it was a severe blow. He was terribly disappointed.

Éric: "How did you react to all of this, François?"

François: "I didn't feel great, as you know. When I find a good ingredient, it's as though there is an explosion in my mind. I see all these different ideas for new desserts that I'm eager to get out there and test. So it is hard when things like this happen."

Éric: "We will surely find other ingredients to inspire you!"

François: "It won't be the same. It's like when something inspires an artist to paint, and then, all of a sudden, the colors disappear from their palette."

THE BIG DAY WAS APPROACHING

It was time to double up our efforts to finish all the recipes we needed for the Grand Central Market Food Truck Festival.

The time had come for last-minute testing and for putting the finishing touches to the dishes. The team was hard at work in the food truck to ensure this trip was a resounding success. In Paris, François works with a team of thirty people, and his main role is to create the pastries and desserts that will be made by them. He was on his own in the food truck, with limited space and materials, unlike his usual working conditions. It required some creative thinking!

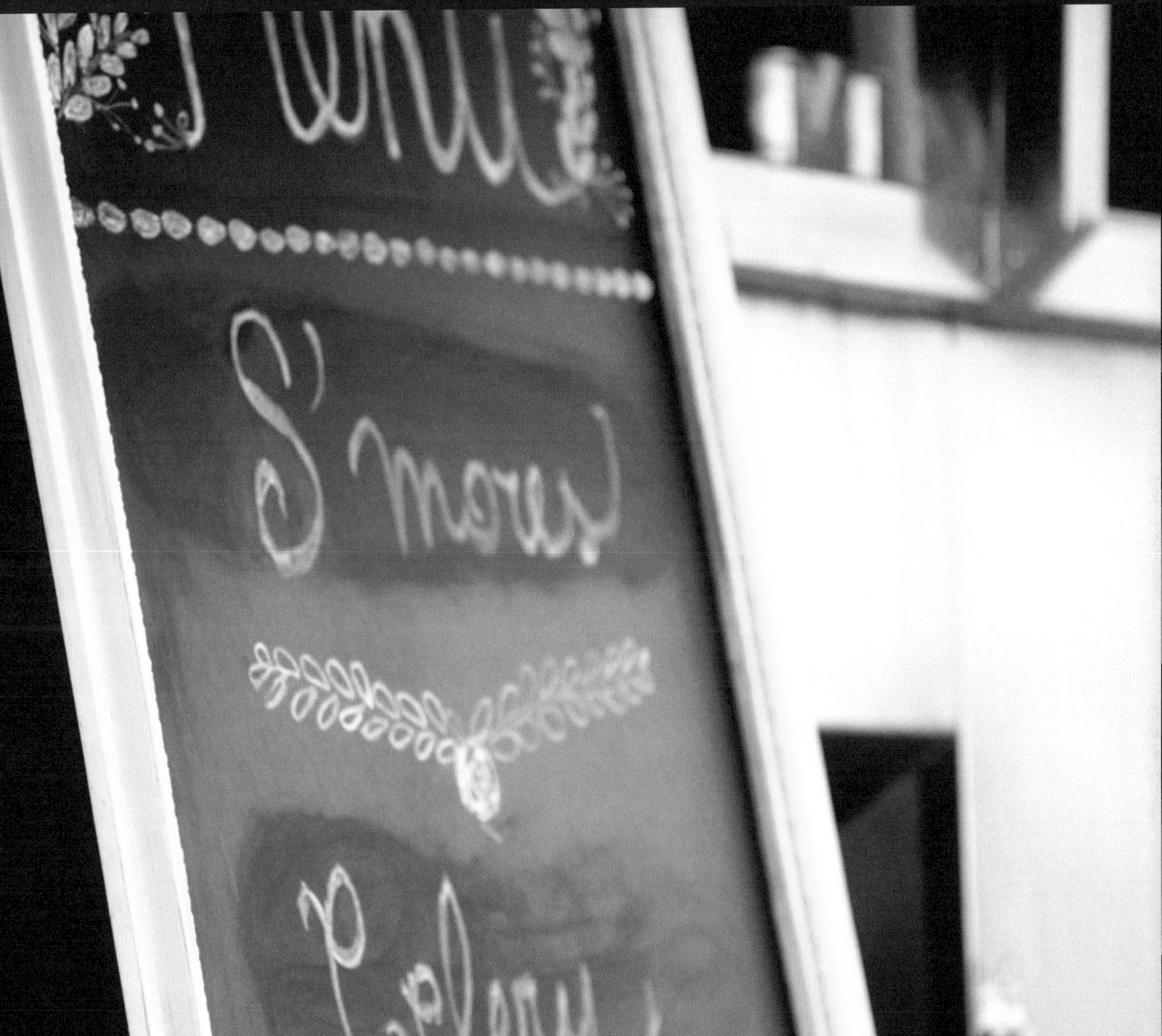
S'mores
Celery

François: "I can finally spend the day experimenting and perfecting these desserts. There is a big culinary fusion movement in France, and I see a big cultural melting pot here in LA, topped with an incredible energy! A constant positive energy that really makes you feel good!"

Éric: "How did this work in such a tight space?"

François: "Well, we needed to adapt! Seeing Teddy work and delegate tasks at the start of this adventure helped me optimize this tiny space."

Éric: "Did you like the challenge?"

François: "I loved it. Cooking in a five-star hotel and cooking in a food truck are the same thing. What counts is your desire to make something good and, more importantly, to make people happy. But what I enjoyed the most was having the possibility to read the customers' reactions in real time, to share their emotions."

Éric: "I think it's about time that we taste all these creations. What do you think?"

François: "I won't let you taste anything until you tell me where you are taking me next time!"

THE LAST STOP

At last, we reached our final destination—The Grand Central Market Food Truck Festival. The Grand Central Market has a long and rich history that forms part of the fabric of the city of LA. It has been operating continuously since it opened in 1917, when Broadway was the main shopping district in Downtown Los Angeles. People from all over the city came to shop in the open-air food hall, and the vendors reflected the neighborhood's demographic makeup, running the gamut from mouthwatering Jewish delis to tasty Mexican taquerias. You can find anything you want here!

Setting up the food truck and preparing everything that was needed were cause for a few final moments of stress, but it was pleasurable all the same. And then we were ready! The hatch of the food truck was opened and over 300 customers came by to test François's new creations, his reinterpretations of classic American desserts. For François, this was no ordinary experience, but the culmination of everything he had been working toward since his arrival in the US.

Éric: "What did you think of our adventure? What will you take back to France with you?"

François: "For one, sincere gratitude that—despite thousands of miles of separation—there are people everywhere who continue to push the limits of the culinary world and who share my passion for pleasing customers. And beyond that, what an experience! Despite some challenges and some desserts that I, personally, didn't particularly like, I felt lucky to be able to experience something new. I can't wait to incorporate these discoveries in my future creations, and—believe it or not—put that much talked-about kumquat dessert on the menu sometime soon."

FRANÇOIS PERRET'S RECIPE JOURNAL

WHISKY BABAS WITH CHANTILLY CREAM

After testing this recipe with different alcohols while we were filming the series, I concluded that I liked whisky best (but I already knew that). I also discovered, thanks to Jade, that gin works well, too. As for Tom, he had a soft spot for tequila. Let your own personal tastes guide you when choosing the right liquor for your babas. For my part, Lagavulin whisky seems perfect and, I thought, why not add a couple of grinds of black pepper and a little grated chocolate as well? If your preference is for gin, try adding lemon zest and maybe some grated root ginger. The choice is yours!

MAKES 8–10

PREPARATION: **2 HOURS** ✳ RESTING: **OVERNIGHT** ✳ COOKING: **35 MINUTES** ✳ LEVEL: **EASY**

INGREDIENTS

Baba dough (make 1 day ahead)
2¼ cups (7 oz./200 g)
  all-purpose flour
¾ tsp (4 g) *fleur de sel* sea salt
4 tsp (20 g) superfine sugar
⅓ oz. (10 g) fresh yeast
2 tsp water
2 large eggs (½ cup/120 g)
¼ cup (2 oz./60 g) unsalted butter,
  diced + extra for the molds

Soaking syrup (make 1 day ahead)
4 cups (1 L) water
2 cups (10½ oz./300 g) light brown
  sugar
Generous ¾ cup (200 ml) whisky
Seeds from 1 vanilla bean

Chantilly cream
1¼ cups (300 ml) whipping cream
  (33% fat)
6 tbsp (1¾ oz./50 g) confectioners'
  sugar, sifted

Glaze (optional)
Apple jelly

To serve
Generous ¾ cup (200 ml) thick
  crème fraiche

→

To prepare the baba dough
Sift the flour into the bowl of the stand mixer and stir in the *fleur de sel* and sugar. Dilute the yeast in the water and add to the bowl, along with the eggs. Mix on low speed until a dough is obtained.

Increase the speed to medium and continue kneading until the dough comes away from the sides of the bowl. Gradually add the butter and knead until the dough comes away from the sides of the bowl again.

Lightly grease the individual baba molds or loaf pan with butter. Divide the dough between the molds (about 1 oz./30 g in each) or place in the loaf pan. Let rise for 15–20 minutes.

Preheat the oven to 300°F (150°C/Gas Mark 2). Bake the babas for 22 minutes, until golden.

Reduce the oven temperature to 250°F (130°C/Gas Mark ½). Unmold the babas and let them dry out in the oven for 13 minutes. This will help them better absorb the syrup.

To prepare the soaking syrup
Heat the water and sugar in a saucepan until the sugar dissolves, then bring to a boil. Let cool until the temperature of the syrup reaches 120°F (50°C). Add the whisky and vanilla bean seeds.

Place the babas in a shallow dish, then pour the syrup over them. Leave overnight in the refrigerator, as the babas must be thoroughly soaked with the syrup. Check the babas the next day and spoon over any syrup that has not been absorbed, if necessary.

To prepare the Chantilly cream
Whip the cream in a well-chilled bowl until it begins to thicken. Add the confectioners' sugar and continue whipping until the cream holds firm peaks. Keep chilled.

→

Equipment

Stand mixer fitted with the dough hook

8–10 individual baba (mini savarin) molds or a loaf pan measuring 10 in. (26 cm) in length

Instant-read thermometer

Electric hand beater

Pastry bag fitted with a ½-in. (1-cm) fluted tip (or whipping siphon)

To glaze (*optional*)

Warm the apple jelly and brush it over the babas.

To assemble

Drain the baba or babas from the dish. If you have chosen to use traditional baba molds, fill the center of each baba with thick crème fraîche. Transfer the Chantilly cream to the pastry bag (or whipping siphon) and decorate with a swirl of cream. For the loaf pan baba, simply spoon over the crème fraîche and serve, with the Chantilly cream on the side.

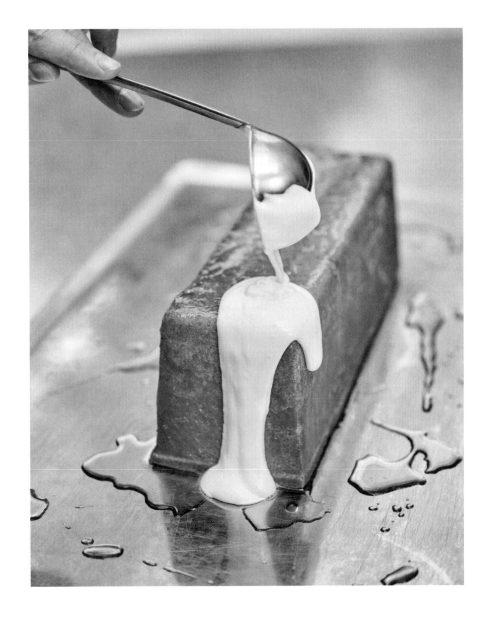

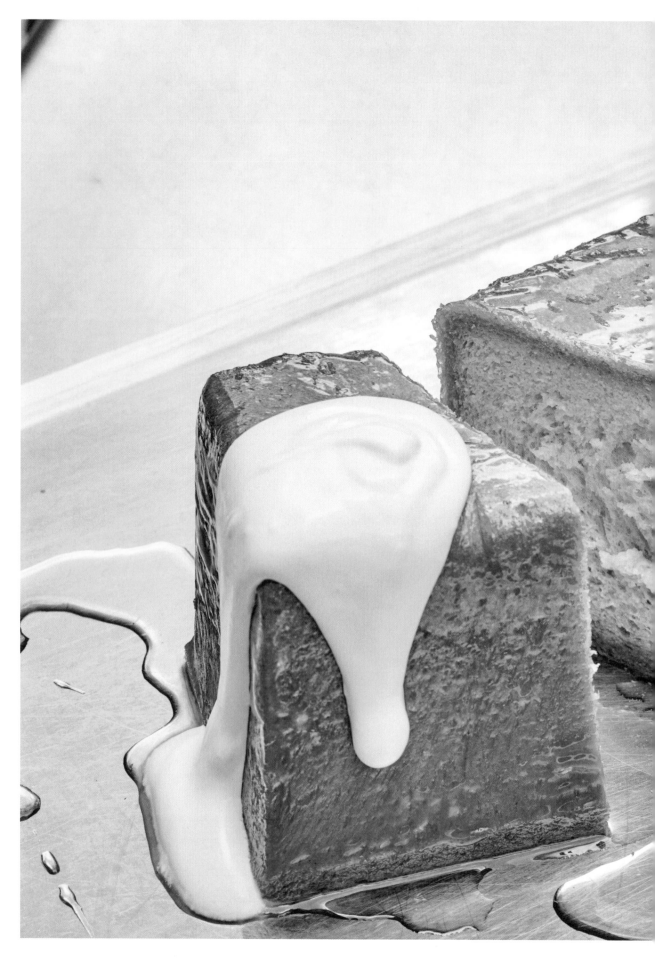

CARROT-SHAPED CARROT CAKE

The key to this recipe is to use small spring carrots with fronds. In the series, I hollowed out the carrots first, but there's really no need to do this, as it's quite fiddly and time-consuming!

SERVES 4–6

PREPARATION: **1½ HOURS** ✳ COOKING: **30 MINUTES** ✳ LEVEL: **INTERMEDIATE**

INGREDIENTS

Carrot cake
Scant ½ cup (3 oz./80 g) superfine
   sugar
2 tbsp (30 g) brown sugar
Generous ¾ cup (3½ oz./100 g)
   all-purpose flour, sifted
1½ tsp baking powder
Scant 1 tsp salt
Heaping 1 tsp unsweetened cocoa
   powder, sifted
Scant 1 tsp ground cinnamon
1 large egg (3½ tbsp/55 g)
⅓ cup (90 ml) grape-seed oil
5½ oz. (150 g) grated carrots

Carrot decoration
1 bunch small spring carrots
   with fronds
1 bunch cilantro

Carrot glaze
1⅓ cups (300 ml) carrot juice
2 tbsp (30 ml) water
1½ tsp (6 g) pectin NH (available
   from specialized food stores
   or on internet)
1 tbsp (12 g) superfine sugar

Cheese cream
Scant ½ cup (3½ oz./100 g) cream
   cheese
3 tbsp (50 ml) whipping cream

Equipment
10-in. (26-cm) cake pan lined with
   parchment paper
Electric hand beater

To prepare the carrot cake
Preheat the oven to 340°F (170°C/Gas Mark 3).

Combine the sugars, flour, baking powder, salt, cocoa powder, and spices in a mixing bowl. Whisk in the egg, then the oil. When the batter is smooth, stir in the grated carrots.

Transfer the batter to the cake pan. Bake for 10–15 minutes, or until the tip of a knife pushed into the center comes out clean.

Turn the cake out onto a wire rack to cool. Once it has cooled, chop it into very small pieces to resemble soil. This will be used as a "bed" for the carrot.

To prepare the carrot decoration
Peel the carrots and cut off their fronds. Use a skewer to make small holes about ½ in. (1 cm) deep in each carrot where the fronds were. Sprigs of cilantro will be "planted" into these holes later.

Steam the carrots for about 10 minutes, checking them toward the end of the cooking time, as they should remain crisp. Set aside.

To prepare the carrot glaze
Heat the carrot juice and water together in a saucepan on medium heat, until the temperature reaches 140°F (60°C). Mix the sugar and pectin together, then add to the hot juice and water. Increase the heat, bring to a boil, and boil for 2 minutes. Let cool, cover, and chill until needed.

Before using the glaze, reheat it gently in the microwave until melted, watching it carefully as it must not boil. The glaze needs to be used melted but cold.

Transfer the cooled, steamed carrots to a wire rack set over a sheet of parchment paper to catch any drips. Spoon a generous amount of glaze over each carrot. Repeat with more glaze, if necessary, until they are all well coated. Place the glazed carrots on a lightly oiled plate and chill until needed.

To prepare the cheese cream
Place the cream cheese in a mixing bowl. Beat in the whipping cream a little at a time to soften it.

→

To assemble

Spoon a little of the cheese cream onto flat individual serving plates. Top with 2 tablespoons of the carrot cake "soil" and carefully shape it into small mounds. Push cilantro sprigs into the small hole made in the top of each carrot to resemble carrot fronds. Divide the carrots between the serving plates, placing them on top of the mounds of "soil."

For a more spectacular presentation, you can also assemble the carrots on a large serving platter. Spoon the cheese cream over the platter, top with the carrot cake "soil," and arrange the glazed carrots on top.

LIKE A COOKIE

The quantities of ingredients for making these cookies are intentionally large. They can be used to make this recipe or simply eaten as cookies. The unbaked dough will freeze well for up to 3 months, which means you can bake a batch of cookies in less time than it would take you to go out and buy some!

SERVES 8

PREPARATION: **1 HOUR** ✳ COOKING: **20 MINUTES** ✳ LEVEL: **INTERMEDIATE**

INGREDIENTS

Cookie dough
1 cup (5 oz./140 g) brown sugar
9 oz. (250 g) butter
¼ cup (1¾ oz./50 g) peanut butter
1 large egg (3½ tbsp/55 g)
2 cups (9 oz./250 g) all-purpose flour
1 tbsp (11 g) baking powder
6½ oz. (180 g) milk chocolate, chopped
6½ oz. (180 g) dark chocolate, 70% cacao, chopped

Pistachio praline
3 tbsp (45 ml) water
4½ oz. (130 g) superfine sugar
7 oz. (200 g) shelled pistachios, skins left on
Generous ⅓ tsp (2 g) *fleur de sel* sea salt
A drizzle of pistachio oil (if required)

Caramelized pistachios
7 oz. (200 g) shelled pistachios, skins left on
1 tbsp (15 ml) water
½ cup (2¾ oz./75 g) brown sugar
Generous ¾ tsp (4 g) *fleur de sel* sea salt
1 tbsp roasted pistachio oil

→

To prepare the cookie dough
Beat the sugar, butter, and peanut butter together in a mixing bowl until light and creamy. Beat in the egg. Sift together the flour and baking powder, and mix in. Stir in the chopped chocolate. Shape the dough into 2 cylinders measuring 12 in. (30 cm) in length. Cover with plastic wrap and freeze until needed.

When ready to bake the cookies, cut the dough into ¾-in. (1.5-cm) thick slices. Preheat the oven to 340°F (170°C/Gas Mark 3). Lay the cookies on a silicone baking mat or cookie sheet lined with parchment paper and bake for 8 minutes. Let cool on a wire rack.

To prepare the pistachio praline
Place the water and sugar in a large saucepan and cook over low heat until the sugar dissolves. Bring to a boil, then continue boiling until the temperature of the syrup reaches 244°F (118°C). Remove from the heat and stir in the pistachios until they are coated, and the mixture has a sandy appearance. Return the saucepan to medium-low heat and cook, stirring constantly, until the sugar caramelizes.

Turn the pistachios out onto a silicone baking mat or lined cookie sheet and sprinkle with the *fleur de sel*. Let cool completely. Once cooled, break into pieces and coarsely grind in a food processor. The praline should have the consistency of pancake batter but retain a granular texture. If necessary, add a little roasted pistachio oil to adjust the consistency.

To prepare the caramelized pistachios
Preheat the oven to 275°F (140°C/Gas Mark 1).

Spread the pistachios over a silicone baking mat or lined cookie sheet and toast them in the oven for 10 minutes. Watch them carefully to ensure they do not burn.

Place the water and sugar in a large saucepan and cook over low heat until the sugar dissolves. Bring to a boil, then continue boiling until the temperature of the syrup reaches 250°F (121°C). Remove from the heat and stir in the hot pistachios until they are coated and the mixture has a sandy appearance. Return the

→

Fromage blanc topping
3 sheets (6 g) gelatin
5 tbsp (75 ml) whole milk
5 tbsp (75 ml) whipping cream
14 oz. (400 g) fromage blanc
    (if unavailable, use quark or
    Greek yogurt)
1 tbsp (15 g) superfine sugar

**Chocolate velvet mixture (see
Chef's Notes)**
10½ oz. (300 g) dark chocolate,
    70% cacao, chopped
10½ oz. (300 g) cocoa butter,
    chopped

To decorate
Roughly chopped chocolate

Equipment
Electric hand beater
Instant-read or candy
    thermometer
Food processor
Whipping siphon fit with a gas
    cartridge
Velvet spray gun
Pastry bag fitted with a large
    plain tip
4¾-in. (12-cm) round cake ring

saucepan to medium-low heat and cook, stirring constantly, until the sugar caramelizes. Add the *fleur de sel* and roasted pistachio oil.

Immediately turn the pistachios out onto a silicone baking mat or cookie sheet lined with parchment paper and separate them using two forks while they are still hot, so they do not stick together.

To prepare the fromage blanc topping
Soak the gelatin in a bowl of cold water until softened. Drain and squeeze to remove excess water. Place in a bowl and microwave on full power for 5 seconds, or until melted. Add the milk, cream, fromage blanc, and sugar to the gelatin and beat together until combined. Transfer the mixture to a whipping siphon fit with a gas cartridge, and refrigerate until needed.

To prepare the chocolate velvet mixture
Melt the chocolate and cocoa butter together in a bowl over a pan of simmering water (bain-marie). Pass through a fine-mesh sieve and transfer to the velvet spray gun. Use at a temperature of 113°F (45°C).

To assemble
Crumble a cookie in the center of each dessert plate. Spoon the pistachio praline into the pastry bag fitted with a large plain tip and pipe a spiral on top of the crumbs. Center the cake ring over the praline. Siphon the fromage blanc topping over the crumbled cookies and praline to cover them completely in an even layer. Carefully remove the ring.

Before spraying with the chocolate velvet mixture, cover the serving plate using a piece of stiff cardboard with a circle the same size as the cake ring cut from the center, to avoid spraying the plate. Spray the warm chocolate velvet mixture directly onto the fromage blanc topping to cover it completely. Hold the spray gun at least 12 in. (30 cm) away and, preferably, do this outdoors (such as a balcony, terrace, backyard or, if you have no outside space, in the bathtub).

Carefully lift the cardboard protection off the plate. Sprinkle over a few caramelized pistachios and a little chopped chocolate to decorate.

Chef's Notes
• Instead of making the chocolate velvet mixture, you can purchase an aerosol can of chocolate spray paint from patisserie supply stores or on the Internet.

CHOCOLATE AND RASPBERRY DONUTS

I find the idea of a flawless trompe-l'oeil donut, made of a sponge cake filled with fruit, glazed with sugar, and cooked without any deep-frying, an extremely interesting one. It makes the perfect accompaniment to a glass of milk or a hot drink. It also contains very little fat: only grape-seed oil, not even butter (yes, for once, I'm not using any butter!).

MAKES 12

PREPARATION: **30 MINUTES** ✳ COOKING: **12 MINUTES** ✳ LEVEL: **EASY**

INGREDIENTS

Chocolate sponge
5 large egg yolks (scant 1½ cups/ 100 g)
½ cup (2 oz./60 g) confectioners' sugar, sifted
4 large egg whites (generous ½ cup/120 g)
5 tbsp (2 oz./60 g) superfine sugar
Scant 1 cup (3½ oz./100 g) all-purpose flour
3½ tbsp (1 oz./25 g) unsweetened cocoa powder

Chocolate glaze
Generous 2 cups (10 oz./280 g) confectioners' sugar
3 tbsp (¾ oz./20 g) unsweetened cocoa powder
5 tbsp (75 ml) water
2½ tbsp (40 ml) grape-seed oil

To assemble
½ pint (6 oz./170 g) fresh raspberries, washed and lightly crushed with a fork
Grated or finely ground dark chocolate

Equipment
Electric hand beater
Pastry bag fitted with a large plain tip
24 × 3-in. (8-cm) silicone savarin molds (or a mold with 24 × 3-in./ 8-cm cavities)
3-in. (8-cm) and 1⅓-in. (3.5-cm) round cookie cutters

To prepare the chocolate sponge

In a large mixing bowl, whisk the egg yolks and confectioners' sugar together until pale and slightly increased in volume. In a separate bowl, whisk the egg whites until they hold soft peaks. Whisk in half the superfine sugar, followed by the other half, continuing to whisk until the egg whites form firm, but not grainy peaks. Using a spatula, gently fold the whisked egg whites into the egg yolk mixture. Sift in the flour and cocoa powder, then carefully fold in until combined.

Preheat the oven to 340°F (170°C/Gas Mark 3).

Transfer the cake batter to the pastry bag fitted with a large plain tip. Grease the silicone savarin molds and pipe the batter into them. Bake for 8–9 minutes, or until a toothpick pushed into one of the sponges comes out clean.

Let cool in the molds. Using a serrated knife, trim their tops level with the tops of the molds. Place in the freezer until firm, then unmold. Neaten the outer edges of the sponges using the 3-in. (8-cm) cookie cutter, and the insides of the rings using the 1⅓-in. (3.5-cm) cutter.

To prepare the chocolate glaze

Sift the confectioners' sugar and cocoa powder into a mixing bowl. Gradually whisk in the water and grape-seed oil until smooth. Set aside at room temperature.

To assemble

Preheat the oven to 425°F (220°C/Gas Mark 7).

Sandwich the sponges together in pairs with the crushed raspberries in the center. Using two forks, dip the donuts in the chocolate glaze to coat them completely. Once dipped, place them on a wire rack set over a cookie sheet to allow excess glaze to drip off.

Place in the oven for 30 seconds to set the glaze. Remove from the oven and sprinkle ground or grated chocolate on top. Bake for an additional 1½ minutes.

Serve warm or at room temperature.

FENNEL SALAD

This is a recipe that was tested in the food truck. At the time, I was not entirely convinced it would work. I didn't think dates or marmalade should be added—or even olives, if my memory serves me right. They can be replaced by a few orange segments instead, resulting in a fresher (and, for me, more enjoyable!) salad. A little *fleur de sel* sea salt and a few turns of the pepper mill will enhance the flavor.

SERVES 4

PREPARATION: **30 MINUTES** ✳ COOKING: **20 MINUTES** ✳ LEVEL: **EASY**

INGREDIENTS

Vinaigrette
Scant ½ cup (100 ml) olive oil
3 tbsp (40 ml) calamansi vinegar
    (or another lemon vinegar)
3 tbsp (40 ml) Pacific (alcohol-free
    pastis)
5 tbsp (40 g) confectioners' sugar

Oat milk rice pudding
1 tbsp (10 g) cornstarch
1 oz. (30 g) light brown sugar
Scant ¾ cup (5½ oz./150 g) risotto
    rice
4 cups (1 L) oat milk

Orange marmalade (optional)
1 lb. (500 g) oranges
1⅓ cups (9 oz./250 g) superfine
    sugar
1 tsp (4 g) fruit pectin (optional,
    but it gives a better set)

Salad
2 fennel bulbs
A little lemon juice
1 lb. (500 g) lemon sorbet
10 pitted dates, thinly sliced
    (optional)
2 large oranges, peeled and
    segmented
20 Taggiasca olives (optional)
1 bunch fresh dill
Borage flowers
Fleur de sel sea salt and freshly
    ground pepper

Equipment
Food processor or blender
Mandoline

To prepare the vinaigrette
Whisk all the ingredients together until evenly combined. Set aside.

To prepare the oat milk rice pudding
Mix the cornstarch and sugar together. Blanch the rice in a saucepan of boiling water for 2 minutes. Drain and rinse under running cold water.

While the rice is blanching, heat the oat milk in a large saucepan until it comes to a simmer. Add the rice and simmer gently over low heat until the rice is tender (about 15 minutes). Stir in the mixture of cornstarch and sugar, then bring briefly to a boil. The rice should be very creamy.

To prepare the orange marmalade
Prick the oranges all over with a fork. Place them in a saucepan with sufficient cold water to cover them and bring to a boil. Drain and repeat 8 times, using fresh water each time.

Cut the oranges into quarters, remove the seeds, and purée in a food processor or blender. Transfer the purée to a saucepan, add the sugar and pectin (if using), and cook for 2 minutes. Let cool.

To assemble
Slice the fennel bulbs very thinly with a mandoline and toss in the lemon juice to stop the slices from oxidizing.

Place a teaspoon of orange marmalade (no more, as it is very sweet) in each serving dish. Add the rice pudding, a scoop of lemon sorbet, and a few date slices (if using).

Divide the fennel slices between the serving dishes, along with the orange segments. Drizzle over the vinaigrette and season with *fleur de sel* and freshly ground pepper.

Served garnished with a few olives (if using), dill sprigs, and borage flowers.

S'MORES POPSICLES

This is the most American of my desserts in form, but equally the most French due to its different components. I have a feeling that this dessert is going to stay with me for a while yet. What's more, it has been a big hit back in Paris. It's simple, yet effective—everything I like.

MAKES ABOUT 40

PREPARATION: **1 HOUR** ✳ COOKING: **30 MINUTES** ✳ FREEZING: **1 HOUR 20 MINUTES MINIMUM** ✳ LEVEL: **EASY**

INGREDIENTS

Crumble topping
¾ stick (2¾ oz. /80 g) butter, softened
Generous ½ cup (2¾ oz./80 g) brown sugar
Generous ¾ cup (3½ oz./100 g) all-purpose flour

Choux pastry
Generous ½ cup (140 ml) whole milk
Generous ½ cup (140 ml) water
1 stick (4 oz./110 g) butter, diced
1 tsp sugar
1 tsp salt
1⅓ cups (6 oz./170 g) all-purpose flour, sifted
4 large eggs (scant 1 cup/200 g), beaten

Frozen mousse
2 large egg whites (¼ cup/60 g)
½ cup (3½ oz./100 g) superfine sugar
Generous ½ cup (150 ml) whipping cream
Scant ¼ cup (50 ml) heavy cream
5 oz. (150 g) dark chocolate, 70% cacao, melted and cooled
2¾ oz. (75 g) dark chocolate, 70% cacao, finely grated

Chocolate coating
10½ oz. (300 g) dark chocolate, 70% cacao, chopped
7 oz. (200 g) cocoa butter, chopped

Meringue
8 large egg whites (1 cup/240 g)
1¼ cups (8½ oz./240 g) superfine sugar

To prepare the crumble topping
Place the softened butter in a mixing bowl. Add the sugar and flour. Work together with your fingers to make a crumble. Press evenly over a board to form a ¹⁄₁₆-in. (2-mm) thick layer. Cut out small circles using the cookie cutter. Set aside.

To prepare the choux pastry
Heat the milk, water, butter, sugar, and salt in a large saucepan until the butter melts and the sugar dissolves. Bring to a boil, take the pan off the heat, and tip in all the flour. Beat vigorously until the batter is smooth and comes away cleanly from the sides of the pan. Transfer the batter to the bowl of the stand mixer. Gradually beat in the eggs on medium speed. The batter needs to be smooth, glossy, and firm enough to hold its shape, so not all of the egg may be needed.

Preheat the oven to 350°F (180°C/Gas Mark 4). Spoon the batter into the pastry bag fitted with a ⅓-in (8-mm) tip and pipe out small mounds measuring 1½ in. (4 cm) in diameter onto silicone baking mats or lined cookie sheets. Leave space between them as they will rise during baking. Carefully place a circle of crumble on top of each choux puff. Bake for about 30 minutes, until golden brown and crisp.

To prepare the frozen mousse
Whisk the egg whites and sugar in a bowl set over a saucepan of barely simmering water (bain-marie) until the mixture is hot but has not exceeded 113°F (45°C). Remove from the saucepan and continue whisking until the egg whites are firm, glossy, and cool.

Whip the creams until they hold soft peaks. Gently fold the melted, cooled chocolate into the meringue, followed by the whipped creams. Lastly, fold in the grated chocolate. Spoon into the pastry bag fitted with a ¼-in. (5-mm) tip.

Pierce a hole in the base of each choux puff and fill with the mousse. Place in the freezer for at least 1 hour, until very firm.

To prepare the chocolate coating
Melt the chocolate and cocoa butter together in a bowl set over a saucepan of barely simmering water (bain-marie) until the temperature reaches 122°F (50°C), stirring until smooth.

→

→

Equipment
1¼-in. (3-cm) cookie cutter
Stand mixer fitted with the whisk
Pastry bag fitted with a ⅓-in
  (8-mm) plain tip
Instant-read thermometer
Electric hand beater
Pastry bag fitted with a ¼-in.
  (5-mm) plain tip
40 wooden popsicle sticks
Styrofoam block
Kitchen torch

To prepare the meringue

Whisk the egg whites until they hold soft peaks. Gradually whisk in the sugar, until the peaks are very stiff and glossy.

To assemble

Remove the choux puffs from the freezer. Push a popsicle stick into the base of each puff, then dip in the chocolate coating. Push the stick into a Styrofoam and let the coating set. Return to the freezer for about 20 minutes. Shortly before serving, dip the puffs in the meringue and place back in the Styrofoam block. To serve, use a kitchen torch to scorch the meringue until lightly golden, in front of your guests. The delicious scent of the toasted meringue will make everyone's mouth water!

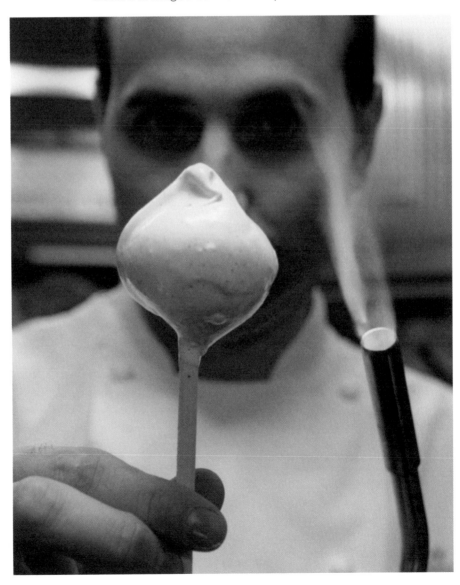

ASPARAGUS TACOS

I love using vegetables in desserts! They offer such an array of possibilities. I sometimes wonder who decreed that fruits should be kept for desserts and vegetables only served earlier in the meal. The tomato is the best example of why this is not actually true: it is a fruit, yet no one is shocked to see it in an appetizer or main dish. A beautifully prepared vegetable deserves to be served for dessert just as much as for the main course. However, a perfect balance must be achieved, as the aim is to surprise diners with the taste.

SERVES 4

PREPARATION: **3 HOURS** ✳ COOKING: **20 MINUTES** ✳ LEVEL: **ADVANCED**

INGREDIENTS

Cracker dough
2 cups (9 oz./250 g) all-purpose
  flour
2½ tbsp (35 ml) olive oil
1 oz. (30 g) fresh yeast
Generous ⅓ cup (100 ml)
  warm water
2 tsp (10 g) *fleur de sel* sea salt

Candied lemons
2 Meyer lemons
1⅔ cups (400 ml) water, divided
1 cup (7 oz./200 g) superfine
  sugar, divided

Poached asparagus
8 large green asparagus spears
2 cups (500 ml) water
½ cup (3½ oz./100 g) sugar
Scant ⅛ tsp salt

Lemon vinaigrette
4 tbsp olive oil
1 tbsp lemon vinegar
1 tbsp confectioners' sugar

Fromage blanc mousse
4½ oz. (125 g) fromage blanc
  (if unavailable, use quark or
  Greek yogurt)
2½ tsp (10 g) superfine sugar
3½ tbsp (50 ml) heavy cream
Scant ⅓ cup (70 ml) whipping
  cream

→

To prepare the cracker dough

In a stand mixer fitted with the dough hook, work the flour and olive oil together until a sandy texture is obtained. Crumble the yeast into the warm water to dissolve and add it to the bowl. Add the salt. Beat on medium speed for 20 minutes. Press plastic wrap over the dough and let rise at room temperature for 30 minutes.

Preheat the oven to 425°F (220°C/Gas Mark 7).

Knead the dough again briefly. Pass it through a dough sheeter, dusting the dough lightly with flour as necessary. Begin on the thickest setting and adjust to a thinner one each time you roll, until the dough is wafer thin (0.8 mm setting). Using a sharp knife, cut the dough into 4- × 1½-in. (10- × 4-cm) rectangles. Arrange the rectangles on a silicone baking mat or lined cookie sheet and place in the oven. Immediately lower the oven temperature to 340°F (170°C/Gas Mark 3) and bake for 6 minutes. Turn the rectangles over and bake for an additional 4–5 minutes, until they are golden.

To prepare the candied lemons

Cut the lemons into 4 or 6, depending on their size. Cut most of the flesh away from the rind to leave just a thin layer of flesh attached. Blanch the lemon rinds 4 times in boiling water, using fresh water each time.

Heat half the water and half the sugar in a saucepan until the sugar dissolves. Bring to a boil and immerse the rinds in the syrup so they are covered, making sure the temperature of the syrup does not exceed 158°F (70°C). When the rinds are tender, drain them and place in a shallow dish. Prepare a second syrup with the rest of the water and sugar and bring to a boil. Pour it over the lemon rinds and cover the dish with plastic wrap.

To prepare the poached asparagus

Cut off the tips of the asparagus stalks to a length of about 1½ in. (4 cm) and set them aside. Using the truffle shaver or mandoline, shave the asparagus stalks into very thin ribbons and place in a saucepan. In a separate saucepan, make a syrup with the water,

→

Hazelnut praline
4 tsp (20 ml) water
⅓ cup (2⅓ oz./65 g) superfine
  sugar
3½ oz. (100 g) hazelnuts
Scant ¼ tsp *fleur de sel* sea salt
A drizzle of hazelnut oil
  (if required)

Toasted hazelnuts
1¾ oz. (50 g) hazelnuts

To serve
Lemon sorbet
Parmesan shavings
Plain yogurt
Finely grated lemon zest

Equipment
Stand mixer fitted with
  the dough hook
Dough sheeter
Instant-read thermometer
Truffle shaver or mandoline
Disposable pastry bag
Food processor

sugar, and salt. Bring the syrup to a boil, then pour over the asparagus ribbons. Poach them for 1–2 minutes. Drain, reserving the syrup for the asparagus tips. Set aside to cool gradually.

Repeat this process twice with the asparagus tips: poach for about 1 minute, drain, reserving the syrup, then let cool. Bring the syrup back to a boil, pour it over the tips, and let cool again. The asparagus tips should be just cooked—firm and tender at the same time.

To prepare the lemon vinaigrette
Whisk together the olive oil, vinegar and sugar. Set aside.

To prepare the fromage blanc mousse
Whisk together the fromage blanc, sugar, and heavy cream until smooth. In a separate bowl, whip the whipping cream until it holds soft peaks. Using a spatula, gently fold the cream into the fromage blanc mixture. Transfer to a disposable pastry bag.

To prepare the hazelnut praline
Place the water and sugar in a large saucepan and cook over low heat until the sugar dissolves. Bring to a boil, then continue boiling until the temperature of the syrup reaches 244°F (118°C). Remove from the heat and stir in the hazelnuts until they are coated, and the mixture has a sandy appearance. Return the saucepan to medium-low heat and cook, stirring constantly, until the sugar caramelizes to a reddish-brown color. Turn the hazelnuts out onto a silicone baking mat or lined cookie sheet and sprinkle with the *fleur de sel*. Let cool completely. Once cooled, break into pieces and coarsely grind in a food processor. The praline should have the consistency of pancake batter but retain a granular texture. If necessary, add a little hazelnut oil to adjust the consistency.

To prepare the toasted hazelnuts
Preheat the oven to 275°F (140°C/Gas mark 1). Spread the hazelnuts over a cookie sheet lined with parchment paper and toast for 30 minutes, checking their color regularly to ensure they do not burn. Let cool, then separate into halves.

To serve
Using a serrated knife, cut a hole lengthwise in the top of each cracker (do this carefully as they are fragile). Snip off the tip of the pastry bag and pipe the fromage blanc mousse into the hole in each taco. Add 2 small scoops of lemon sorbet. Arrange 2 asparagus tips, halved lengthwise, attractively on top and several asparagus ribbons (at least 8 per serving). Garnish each taco with 4 pieces of candied lemon, a few toasted hazelnut halves, and 3 Parmesan shavings. Drizzle over the hazelnut praline and lemon vinaigrette, and add a little yogurt for a gourmet touch. Finally, grate a little lemon zest over the dessert.

CORN TACOS

This recipe was perfect for cooking in the food truck, directly on the grill plates. I could have added so many other things—go for whatever fillings take your fancy!

SERVES 10

PREPARATION: **1½ HOURS** ✳ RESTING: **OVERNIGHT + 2–2½ HOURS**
COOKING: **40 MINUTES–1½ HOURS** ✳ LEVEL: **ADVANCED**

INGREDIENTS

Brioche (make 1 day ahead)
½ oz. (12 g) fresh yeast
4 tsp (20 ml) milk
3¼ cups (14 oz./400 g) bread flour
1 tbsp (15 g) *fleur de sel* sea salt
4 tbsp (50 g) superfine sugar
4 extra-large eggs (1 cup/250 g)
2½ sticks (10 oz./280 g) unsalted
   butter, diced and softened
1 beaten egg, for glazing
   (optional)

**Candied piquillo peppers
(make 1 day ahead)**
1¾ cups (9 oz./250 g) superfine
   sugar, divided
½ cup (125 ml) water
⅓ tsp (2 g) *Espelette* pepper
1 jar piquillo peppers

Poached corn
3 corn cobs
2 cups (500 ml) whole milk

Puréed corn
2½ cups (12¾ oz./360 g) poached
   corn (see above), drained
4 tbsp (60 ml) poaching liquid
   (see above)

Creamed corn
3 oz. (80 g) puréed corn (see
   above)
1½ oz. (40 g) mascarpone
2 pinches fine salt
Freshly ground pepper

Caramel Sauce
Scant ⅔ cup (4½ oz./125 g)
   superfine sugar
5 tbsp (75 ml) hot water

→

To prepare the brioche

In the bowl of the stand mixer fitted with the dough hook, crumble the yeast into the milk to dissolve it. Add the flour, salt, sugar, and 3 of the eggs. Knead on low speed for 10 minutes. Add the remaining egg and continue kneading on low speed until the dough pulls away cleanly from the sides of the bowl. Gradually add the butter and continue kneading on low speed until the dough is smooth and elastic.

Transfer the dough to another bowl, cover with plastic wrap, and let rest in the refrigerator for 1 hour. Push the dough down and fold it over to prevent it from rising further. Cover tightly in plastic wrap and let rest again in the refrigerator for 1 hour. You now have two options:

Option 1: Make 2 large brioches in the loaf pans. Roll the dough into 12 × 3-oz. (80-g) balls and arrange them close together in staggered rows in the pans, with the seam of each ball facing downward against the base of the pan. Press down lightly on the top of each ball of dough to flatten it slightly. Let rise at room temperature.

Preheat the oven to 300°F (150°C/Gas Mark 2). Brush the top of the dough with beaten egg to glaze, then bake for 45 minutes.

The next day, cut the brioche into very thin slices, then cut out 10 disks using the cookie cutter.

Option 2: Refrigerate the dough overnight. The next day, divide the dough into sections and work one section at a time, keeping the remaining dough chilled. Roll each one briefly several times, placing it back in the refrigerator each time to ensure that it remains well chilled while it is being worked, until it is 1/16 in. (2 mm) thick. Cut out 10 disks using the cookie cutter and place them between two lightly oiled parchment paper sheets. Let rest at room temperature for 25 minutes.

To prepare the candied piquillo peppers

Make a syrup by heating half of the sugar with ½ cup (125 ml) water. Add the *Espelette* pepper, then bring to a boil. Remove from the heat, cover, and let infuse for 5 minutes. Strain through a fine-mesh sieve over the piquillo peppers. Set aside.

The next day, drain the syrup into a saucepan and add the remaining sugar. Bring to a boil, then pour over the piquillo peppers. Set aside.

→

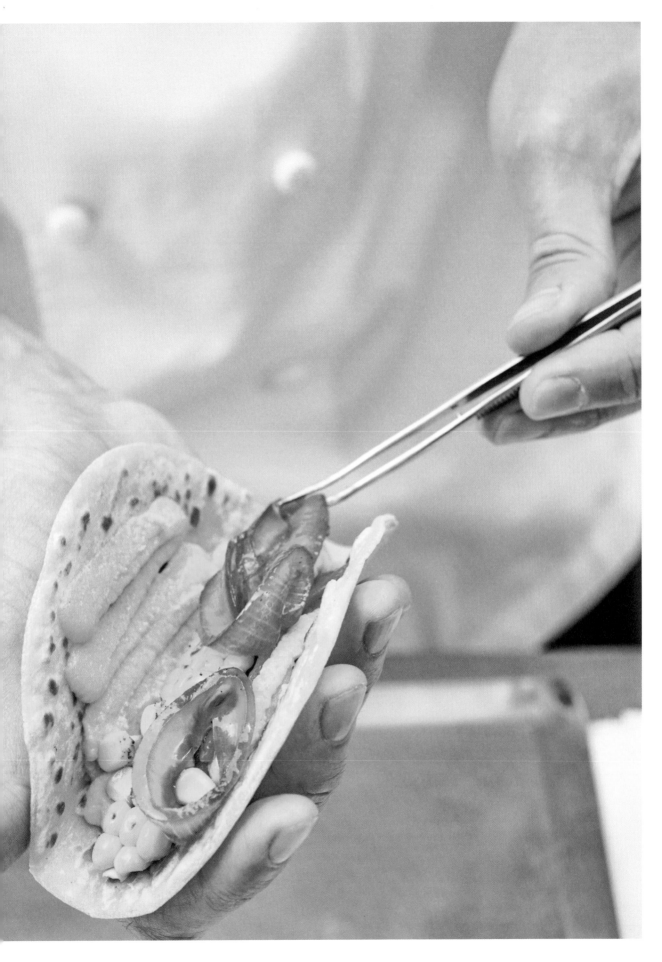

To garnish and serve
1 corn cob
A little vegetable oil
4 small spring onions
Arugula or frisée lettuce
  leaves
Caramel popcorn
Fleur de sel sea salt and freshly
  ground pepper

Equipment
Stand mixer fitted with the dough
  hook
2 loaf pans measuring 9½ × 3 in.
  (24 × 8 cm), if using option 1
6¼-in. (16-cm) cookie cutter
Thermomix or spice grinder (or
  blender)
Pastry bag fitted with a small plain
  round tip
Plancha grill plate (optional)

To prepare the poached corn
Use a sharp knife to cut the corn kernels off the cob. Heat the milk in a saucepan until it comes to a simmer, then add the corn. Cook over low heat until the corn is tender.

To prepare the puréed corn
Place the poached corn and the poaching liquid in the Thermomix or spice grinder (or blender). Blend until smooth. Strain to obtain a thick purée.

To prepare the creamed corn
Place the puréed corn in a mixing bowl and gradually whisk in the mascarpone until smooth. Season with salt and 2 turns of the pepper mill. Transfer the mixture to the pastry bag.

To prepare the caramel sauce
Make a dry caramel by heating the sugar over low heat in a heavy-based saucepan, without adding water. Once the sugar dissolves to form a syrup, boil it until it becomes a golden-brown caramel and the temperature reaches a maximum of 340°F (170°C).

Take the pan off the heat and very carefully deglaze by pouring the hot water over the caramel and swirling the pan. Keep warm.

To prepare the garnish
Use a sharp knife to cut large strips of corn lengthwise off the cob, ensuring that the strips are just thick enough for the kernels to remain joined together. Add a little oil to a skillet and sear the corn strips until lightly browned. Season with *fleur de sel* and pepper.

Cut the spring onions into ¼-in. (5-mm) slices and steam them for about 10 minutes. They should be slightly translucent but still hold their shape. Transfer to a heatproof container and pour over the hot caramel. Cover and set aside.

To serve
Add a little oil to a skillet and, with the stove set to two-thirds of its maximum heat, or ideally on a plancha grill plate, toast or cook the brioche disks until nicely browned underneath. Turn them over to brown the other side.

Once the brioche disks have been toasted or cooked, place the fillings over one half of each round so it can be folded in half once assembled. First add the candied peppers and pipe over the creamed corn. Add the pan-seared corn, the caramel-coated spring onions, 1 or 2 arugula or frisée lettuce leaves, and scatter over some caramel popcorn. Season with a little *fleur de sel* and freshly ground pepper. Fold in half and enjoy!

PEAR TACOS WITH AVOCADO HONEY

This dessert is extremely refreshing thanks to the pears and the superb, but little known, avocado honey, with its bold flavor similar to molasses. Throw in crunchy almonds and crisp *langue de chat* waffles, and you've got yourself a dessert that is both crispy and melt-in-the-mouth—just how I like them! And I find that eating with your fingers—picking up the food and putting it directly into your mouth—is even more pleasurable than using a knife and fork. Long live finger food!

SERVES 8

PREPARATION: **1½ HOURS** ✳ RESTING: **OVERNIGHT** ✳ COOKING: **12 MINUTES** ✳ LEVEL: **INTERMEDIATE**

INGREDIENTS

Fromage blanc mousse (make 1 day ahead)
1 sheet (2 g) gelatin
Generous ¾ cup (7 oz./200 g) fromage blanc (if unavailable, use quark or Greek yogurt)
5 tsp (20 g) superfine sugar
Generous ¾ cup (200 ml) crème fraiche

Langue de chat waffle batter
5½ tbsp (80 g) unsalted butter
¾ cup (3½ oz./100 g) confectioners' sugar
Generous ¾ cup (3½ oz./100 g) all-purpose flour
½ tsp salt
Scant ½ cup (3½ oz./100 g) egg whites

Caramelized almonds
1 cup (7 oz./200 g) almonds
2 tbsp water
½ cup (2½ oz./75 g) light brown sugar
1 tsp *fleur de sel* sea salt
A drizzle of roasted almond oil

To assemble
4 large, perfectly ripe Williams or Bartlett pears, preferably red
Avocado honey for drizzling

→

To prepare the fromage blanc mousse
Soak the gelatin in a bowl of cold water until softened. Drain and squeeze to remove excess water. Place in a bowl and microwave on full power for 5 seconds, or until melted. Whisk together the fromage blanc and sugar until combined, then add the melted gelatin.

In a separate bowl, whip the crème fraiche on low speed until it thickens a little, taking care not to over whip as it will separate easily; it should remain soft and smooth. Gently fold the two mixtures together using a flexible spatula. Transfer to a disposable pastry bag and keep chilled.

To prepare the *langue de chat* waffle batter
Beat the butter in a mixing bowl to soften it. Add the confectioners' sugar and beat until smooth and creamy. Sift in the flour and salt and stir to combine, then whisk in the egg whites.

Preheat the oven to 340°F (170°C/Gas Mark 3). Place the honeycomb-patterned silicone mat on a cookie sheet. Using an offset spatula, spread the batter in an even layer over the silicone mat. Bake for about 10 minutes. Release the batter edges from the silicone mat as soon as they begin to color. Return to the oven for a few minutes, then turn over onto the hot cookie sheet and remove the silicone mat.

Using the cookie cutter, cut out 16 circles (you will need 2 for each taco). Return the waffles to the oven in small batches and bake until they are golden brown. Remove from the oven and immediately place the waffles in the bottom of the 6⅓-in. (16-cm) bowl, pressing down lightly so they cool in a curved shape. Once cooled, carefully remove them from the bowl and store in an airtight container until needed.

To prepare the caramelized almonds
Preheat the oven to 275°F (140°C/Gas Mark 1). Spread the almonds over a cookie sheet lined with parchment paper and

→

Equipment
Electric hand beater
Disposable pastry bag
Silicone baking mat imprinted
  with a honeycomb pattern
4¾-in. (12-cm) cookie cutter
6⅓-in. (16-cm) bowl
Instant-read or candy
  thermometer

toast them in the oven for 10 minutes, watching them carefully so they do not color too much.

Place the water and sugar in a large saucepan and cook over low heat until the sugar dissolves. Bring to a boil, then continue boiling until the temperature of the syrup reaches 250°F (121°C). Remove from the heat and stir in the hot almonds until they are coated, and the mixture has a sandy appearance. Return the saucepan to medium-low heat and cook, stirring constantly, until the sugar caramelizes. Add the *fleur de sel* and roasted almond oil.

Immediately turn the almonds out onto a silicone baking mat or lined cookie sheet. Using two forks, separate them while they are still hot, so they do not stick together.

To assemble

Cut two large round slices, about ⅔ in. (1.5 cm) thick, from each pear, without peeling the fruit. Use the rest of the pears to make a compote (or eat them while you are cooking!). You can also cut the pears into neat cubes measuring at least ½ in. (1.2 cm).

Arrange 8 waffles on a serving platter. Snip off the tip of the pastry bag and pipe a little fromage blanc mousse into the center of each waffle. Place a pear slice or cubes on top. Roughly chop the caramelized almonds, then sprinkle the equivalent of about 5 almonds over each taco. Cover with more mousse and place a second waffle on top.

Drizzle the honey over the tacos in front of your guests—an extremely enticing act that cannot fail to whet the appetite. After all, this dish is all about indulgence!

THE KUMQUAT

This is how I dreamed of preparing this fruit—but we'll make it happen one day, right Éric?

SERVES 4

PREPARATION: **2 HOURS** ✳ RESTING: **OVERNIGHT** ✳ COOKING: **1 HOUR** ✳ LEVEL: **EASY**

INGREDIENTS

Blanched kumquats (make 1 day ahead)
16 very large kumquats (the size of
  small kiwi fruit)

→

To blanch the kumquats

Insert a toothpick into each kumquat, pushing it all the way through. Blanch the kumquats 3 times in boiling water, draining and using fresh water each time (this helps remove some of the bitterness from the kumquat flesh). Remove the toothpicks.

→

Poaching and soaking syrups (make 1 day ahead):

Mandarin orange poaching syrup
4 cups (1 L) water
1 Madagascar bourbon vanilla
   bean
1¼ cups (300 ml) mandarin orange
   juice
1½ cups (10½ oz./300 g) superfine
   sugar

Brown sugar soaking syrup
1¼ cups (300 ml) water
2 cups (10½ oz./300 g) brown
   sugar

Kumquat compote
Reserved kumquat pulp and bases
   (see above)
Brown sugar (¼ of the weight of
   the kumquats)

Clementine sauce
5 tbsp (2 oz./60 g) superfine sugar
½ cup (125 ml) mandarin orange
   poaching syrup (see above)
Juice of 1 lemon
Finely grated zest of 1 clementine
1½ tsp (5 g) cornstarch + 1 tsp
   mandarin orange poaching
   syrup (see above)

To garnish
2 ripe Hass avocados
   (3½ oz./100 g each)
3 tbsp (1 oz./30 g) sesame seeds,
   toasted or seasoned with wasabi
Generous ¾ cup (200 ml)
   whipping cream

Equipment
Toothpicks
Instant-read or candy
   thermometer
Electric beater

To prepare the mandarin orange poaching syrup
Heat the water, vanilla bean, mandarin orange juice, and sugar in a saucepan until the sugar dissolves. Bring the syrup almost to a simmer, add the kumquats, and poach for 25 minutes at 194°F (90°C). Drain, reserving the syrup to make the clementine sauce.

Slice off the base of each kumquat and reserve. Using a teaspoon, scoop out the pulp. Reserve the pulp and place the hollowed-out shells in a bowl.

To prepare the brown sugar soaking syrup
Heat the water and sugar in a saucepan until the sugar dissolves. Bring to a boil and pour over the kumquat shells in the bowl. Cover and let rest overnight.

To prepare the kumquat compote
The next day, remove the seeds from the kumquat pulp and finely chop the reserved bases. Weigh out ¼ of the weight of the pulp and bases in brown sugar, place in a saucepan with the pulp and finely chopped bases, and mix together. Bring to a boil, then let boil for about 3 minutes, stirring constantly. Cool, cover, and refrigerate until needed.

To prepare the clementine sauce
Make a dry caramel by heating the sugar over low heat in a heavy-based saucepan, without adding water. Once the sugar dissolves to form a syrup, boil it until it becomes a golden-brown caramel and the temperature reaches a maximum of 340°F (170°C).

Take the pan off the heat and very carefully deglaze with ½ cup (125 ml) of the reserved mandarin orange poaching syrup, the lemon juice, and the clementine zest. Mix the cornstarch with 1 tsp syrup until smooth, then whisk into the sauce. Stir over medium heat until the sauce comes to a boil. Remove from the heat, press plastic wrap over the surface, and let cool. Refrigerate until needed.

To prepare the garnish
Halve the avocadoes, remove the pits, and cut the flesh into ⅓-in. (1-cm) cubes. Fold the diced avocado and sesame seeds into the kumquat compote until evenly combined.

Lightly whip the cream until it just holds its shape.

To assemble
Place the poached kumquat shells upright and fill each one with a little whipped cream, then the kumquat compote and avocado mixture. Place them upside down on serving plates, drizzle over the clementine sauce, and enjoy!

François Perret and Éric Nebot wish to thank:

Ryma Bouzid and all the staff at Flammarion

Chloé Benitah
Alexander Wolf for his invaluable assistance
Stéphane Reynaud

The teams at the Ritz Paris:
The Fayed family, Natalie Bader, Marc Raffray, Mélanie Hubert,
Silvia Vigneux, Adeline Robinault, Clément Tilly, Julien Loubere, Stéphane Ollivier,
Joris Theysset, the whole team of pâtissiers who work tirelessly, day in, day out,
to turn François's wildest ideas into reality, and all the collaborators at this prestigious
establishment

Their partners, Aurelie Martin and Eleonore Nebot,
and children, Cleo, Tom, Eliezer, and Émile

Their parents and grandparents: Mémé Marie, Pépé Maxime, Mamie Bibine,
Papi Césaire, Mamie Michel, and Papou Robert,
who inspired Éric to want to recount stories

Camille Chambault and the entire film crew of the TV series
The Chef in a Truck, as well as the fantastic directors of photography, Lubomir Bakchev
and Théo Reynal, and film editors, Alex Westphal and Alexandre Donot

The Wild Bunch team

Julien Benhamou, Marc-Antoine Dolfi, Anne-Benedicte Quilici, Gregory Strouk,
Richard Pommerat, Patrick Long, David Nataf, Matthieu Goffard, David Gitlis,
Philippe Simon, Alice Cointe, Élodie Ichou, and everyone at Hill Valley

Jason Neroni and the staff at The Rose Venice, Courtney Cowan
and the team at Milk Jar Cookies, Teddy Vazquez and his tacos, and Thomas Zachariou
and Jade Verdeuil—François's two commis on the show

Pierre Hermé, Pierre Gagnaire, Dominique Ansel, Michel Troisgros, Niki Nakayama,
Gerardo Madrazo, French bakery The Place to Be in Santa Monica,
and its adorable owners, Sandra and Matthieu Guertin

And last but not least, you foodies, who bring to life the passion we wished to share
through this TV series and book, without whom our jobs as pastry chef
and storyteller would have decidedly less flavor.